1

MW01103807

Your Toe

IT COULD BE
THE **LAST** THING
YOU EVER DO

TODD FRIEL

GOSPEL
PARTNERS
MEDIA
Reaching the lost. Together.

Don't Stub Your Toe

Published by
Gospel Partners Media
3070 Windward Plaza, Ste. F301
Alpharetta, GA 30005

Design and production by Genesis Group

Printed in India

ISBN 978-0-9996056-0-8

Reprinted August 2024

You Are Not Lucky Primordial Soup

Despite what you have been told in science class, you are not here by accident; time and chance have not determined your existence.

Are you willing to be open-minded enough to consider an option that is both true and better? Here it is: You were created by God, and for God.[1] You are an image bearer of the Maker of heaven and earth. And that explains why you are the way you are.

You see, every created object reflects aspects of its creator. You are no different. Just as art is a faint reflection of the artist, and a building reflects something of the architect, you bear a resemblance to the God who created you.[2]

- You live because God is alive.

- You think because God thinks.

- You work because God is at work.

Design reveals something about the designer. Your designer is the God of the Bible. While you are not a god, you are made in the likeness of God Himself and you share some of His attributes.

- You see and hear because God sees and hears.

- You communicate because God communicates.

- You have emotions because God has emotions.

Not only has the Creator of the universe intricately designed you, He thought of you before time began, and He knows you even better than you know yourself.[3] God knows your birth date, death date, and every date in between. He sustains your life and is intimately involved in every detail.

Your God, whether you acknowledge Him as such or not, knows what you are going to think, speak, and do before you do. Absolutely nothing about you is a secret to Him. That raises a question: what exactly does He see when He looks at you?

Twenty-five years ago, I would have answered that question the same way you probably did: "Overall, God sees me as a pretty good person." Will you permit me to challenge your answer? You do not need to pass your paper to the front of the class; this is strictly between you and God.

Are You Sure You Are a Good Person?

While this might sound counterintuitive, the most horrifying sentence you will ever hear is, "God is good." God is thoroughly righteous, holy, just, and loving. While that sounds like good news, if we consider this more deeply, it is not good news for us at all.

Because God is good, He loves everything that is good: kindness, generosity, love, faithfulness, patience, grace, mercy, charity, gentleness, compassion, honesty, etc.

Because God loves all things that are good, He necessarily hates everything that is not good: cruelty, murder, theft, violence, hatred, lying, greed, bullying, immorality, unrighteous anger, etc.

God did not write the standard of right and wrong; He is the standard of right and wrong. Morality did not evolve, it exists because God is moral, and our programmer has hardwired us with His moral code. We have a name for that: the conscience.

This explains why you and I feel guilty when we do something wrong. This also explains why you and I have an intuitive fear of death; we sense that something bad could happen on the other side. There is a reason for that too.

Because the foundation of God's throne is righteousness and justice,[4] God cannot and will not let unrighteous acts go unpunished.

- We have courtrooms because God is going to have a day in court with every human who has ever lived.[5]

- We have judges because God is the ultimate supreme court justice.

- We have prisons because God has an eternal prison prepared for lawbreakers.

"It is appointed for men to die once and after this comes judgment."[6] Unlike earthly courts where clever lawyers can manipulate the laws, God will not be fooled. There will be no lost evidence, no perjury, and no confusion.

- Every dirty fantasy will be revealed.

- Every mean thought will be exposed.

- Every deed done in darkness will be brought into the light.

- Every violation of God's perfect, holy law will be judged for what it is: sin.

While this might make you uncomfortable, isn't it better to examine yourself today, rather than wait until it is too late to do anything about it? So let's go to the courtroom of God's justice and see how you will do.

The Court Room

Imagine you are standing before your Creator. The One who spoke the universe into existence opens the books to the pages that bear your name. Your record of lawbreaking is chronicled in perfect detail. Permit me to open the books to just five of God's laws.

First Commandment: "You shall have no other gods before Me"[7]

It is only right that our primary affections go to the One who made us. When we love anything more than God (even good things), those objects effectively become our idols.

Should we love our spouse and children? Yes. Can we enjoy a good meal or own a nice home? Of course. But when we love the gifts more than the Giver, then we have violated this commandment. Can any of us say that our primary affections have always been directed toward the God who made us?

Third Commandment: "You shall not take the name of God in vain"[8]

Have you ever used God's name flippantly, as in "OMG"? Instead of using a four-letter filth word, have you used God's holy name to curse or express disgust? Is it any wonder God says, "The LORD will not leave him unpunished who takes His name in vain"[9]?

Fifth Commandment: "Honor your father and your mother"[10]

Did you always happily obey and honor your parents? Were you ever disobedient or disrespectful? You and I were no different than the little monster children we see at a McDonald's Playland. Every person on the planet has broken this law, including you.

Sixth Commandment: "You shall not murder"[11]

Undoubtedly you think you are safe on this one, but Jesus said, "Everyone who is angry with his brother shall be guilty before the court . . . and whoever says, 'You fool,' shall be guilty enough to go into the fiery hell."[12]

The Bible says that "everyone who hates his brother is a murderer."[13] How many times did you call your siblings names? Have you ever been mad at another driver? Have you ever gossiped and impugned another's reputation? Then God views you as a murderer at heart, because He sees more than our actions; He sees our thought life.

Seventh Commandment: "You shall not commit adultery"[14]

Perhaps you are relieved that you have never had an affair. Read these words of Jesus carefully:

> "You have heard that it was said, 'YOU SHALL NOT COMMIT ADULTERY'; but I say to you that everyone who looks at a woman with lust for her has already committed adultery with her in his heart."[15]

How many sexual thoughts have you had that you would prefer your mother didn't know about? How many times have you stared at pornography? God has recorded every sinful sexual thought you have ever had.

How Did You Do?

That was just five of the Ten Commandments. If you have broken any of God's laws, then you are just like the rest of us: a sinner who has rebelled against the sovereign King of creation.

- We feel guilty because we are guilty.

- We feel shame because we have done shameful things.

- We are afraid to die because our consciences tell us we are in big trouble with our Maker.

When we take inventory of our violations against God's law, we see that we have a warehouse full of sins. Our day in court looks rather bleak.

Objection!

There you are, standing before God with no loved ones, no lawyer, and no excuses. The all-knowing Judge of the world not only heard the evidence of your crimes; He is an eyewitness to your lawbreaking. You and I are guilty beyond the shadow of a doubt.

The King of kings is about to bring down the mallet of His justice and pass sentence. If you are guilty, you will be sent to an eternity in God's prison—a very real place called hell. Your fate is about to be decided and there are no appeals. As God prepares to render your eternal verdict, you feel a desperate need to plead your case.

"Objection, Your Honor, I didn't know You existed."

God has made it abundantly clear that He exists.

- Every human intuitively knows there is an afterlife.[16]

- God has hardwired humans to innately know He exists.[17]

- In creating the universe, God has made His presence inexcusably obvious.[18]

- God has given us a conscience to know we have sinned against our Maker.[19]

When we claim that God doesn't exist, we are merely suppressing the obvious truth, "because that which is known about God is evident within them; for God made it evident to them."[20]

Objection overruled.

"Objection, Your Honor, I'm not as bad as other people."

Michael Ross, known as the Roadside Strangler, murdered eight teens and young women between 1981 and 1984. In an interview before his execution in 2005, he said, "I'm not a big serial killer by the way. Eight people—that's nothing. There's a lot of other guys you can go see."[21] In other words, if you think I am a bad murderer, there are a lot of other serial killers who are worse than me.

Just like Michael Ross, we deceive ourselves when we think we are okay because we are not as bad as other people. That is why the Bible says, "The heart is more deceitful than all else and is desperately sick; who can understand it?"[22]

You think you are not as bad as a crackhead, the crackhead thinks he is better than his dealer, the dealer thinks he is better than the rapist, the rapist thinks he is not as bad as Charles Manson, and Charles Manson thinks he is better than Genghis Khan. Unfortunately, the standard by which we will be judged is God's holy standard, not our own standard.

Imagine a man who embezzled two million dollars saying to a judge, "Your Honor, I know I stole two million, but Bernie Madoff embezzled $65 billion." Now imagine if the judge said, "I never thought of that; you are free to go." If you think that is too ridiculous to be true, you are correct.

Your objection is overruled and God is now prepared to sentence you.

"Objection, Your Honor, I've done good things."

You are not the first person to think your good deeds will outweigh your bad. But the question is not whether a criminal has done anything good; it's whether he has broken the law.

If your son hit his sister in the eye, would you let him off the hook because he made his bed that morning? His "good deeds" do not offset his crimes.

Imagine a criminal who said, "Judge, I murdered my wife, but I washed your car windows on the way into court." That has nothing to do with his crime. A good judge will not only disdain the criminal's bribery, he would be offended. Just like God.

God dismisses your objection and is now prepared to render His verdict.

"Objection, Your Honor, You should let me go because You are good."

Let's say your neighbor committed horrendous crimes, stood in court and pleaded, "Judge, I know I am guilty, but I think you are a really good man and you should overlook my offenses."

The judge would say, "I am indeed good, and that is precisely why I must punish you for your crimes. Because I am good, I am going to give you exactly what you deserve."

"Objection, Your Honor, I haven't committed a lot of sins."

It takes only one criminal act to make a person a criminal; and it takes only one violation of God's commandments to be considered a lawbreaker.[23] But truthfully, who of us can say we haven't committed tons of sins?

Is it fair to say that you have committed at least three sins per day since you were old enough to know what sin is, say, 15 years of age? Let's do some math.

Present age	Total # of years sinning	Total # of sins
20	5	5,475
30	15	16,425
40	25	27,375
50	35	38,325
60	45	49,275
70	55	60,225

As you can see, you have committed a staggering number of crimes against God. If God let a criminal like you go free, He would not be good at all; He would be wicked. And He isn't.

"Objection, Your Honor, I haven't committed any big sins like rape or murder."

While that may be the case, what makes our "little sins" damnable is not the nature of the sin per se, but the One against whom the sin has been committed.

Think of it like this: if I tell a lie to my teenaged son, nothing is going to happen to me. If I lie to my wife, I sleep on the couch. If

I lie to my boss, I get fired. If I lie to the government, I could go to jail. Same crime, different punishment. Why? Because of the one against whom I have committed the crime.

You may think you have committed little sins, but those little offenses have been committed against a supremely holy and righteous God. That offended deity is not persuaded by your objection.

"Objection, Your Honor, an eternity in hell is unreasonable."

It is obvious to everyone but ourselves that eternity in hell is the correct sentence for lawbreakers. A preacher once said, "The moment when you take your first step through the gates of hell, the only thing you will hear is all of creation standing to its feet and applauding and praising God because God has rid the earth of you. That's how not good you are."

You and I minimize our sins because we cannot see ourselves clearly. We are so entangled in sin that we don't realize how wicked we are. The sinless Creator is the One best able to determine the punishment for guilty criminals, not the criminals themselves.

Not only does God see sin as exceedingly sinful, He is the One against whom each and every offense is primarily committed. If anyone should be angry about sin, it is God Himself. And He is. And that anger will last for an eternity.

"Objection, Your Honor, you are too loving to send me to hell."

Imagine a son who broke many laws and found himself in the courtroom of his father, the judge. How would you feel if the judge dismissed his guilty son's case because the child pleaded, "Daddy, if you love me you will let me go."

Perhaps it would be loving toward the child if the father set him free, but it would not be loving toward everyone else. God's holiness demands that justice is served, and that is the most loving thing He could do.

You are out of excuses and objections.

The Inevitable Verdict

There is one word you do not want to hear thundered from God's bench: "Guilty." But that is precisely what God will say to all criminals with a rap sheet. If you think I am trying to scare you, well, you are right. My friend, you should be afraid. "It is a terrifying thing to fall into the hands of the living God."[24]

When God makes His irrevocable decision and slams down His gavel of justice, your eternal fate will be sealed. Isn't it better to know what your verdict will be before it is too late?

If God finds you guilty, and He will, you will be instantly whisked off to God's eternal prison, hell. This is your final resting place, but there will be no rest. God's righteous, holy, indignant wrath will rest on you for all of eternity.

Your first day of activities involves weeping, gnashing your teeth, and torment.[25] Your ten-thousandth day is no different from your first; your suffering will never decrease in intensity. You would give anything for a drop of water or a ray of sunshine, but it never comes. Ever.

You will find no comfort in being surrounded with friends. Hell will not be an eternal party; it will be eternal punishment. And the One inflicting the punishment will be the One against whom you have committed all of your crimes: God Himself.

God, the just judge of the entire world, is going to judge you, and He is willing and able to pour out His anger and wrath on you forever and ever and ever.[26] His holiness, righteousness, and love demand it.

You will receive only ongoing, unrelenting, and intense misery—eternal, conscious torment with no reprieve. You will forever receive the just reward for the unrighteous life you have willingly and knowingly lived.

Is there any hope for sinners like you and me? Is there any way we can escape the horrors of hell?

It Is Not Too Late

One of the best words in the Bible is "but." You and I are lawbreakers who have earned an eternity of God's wrath... *but*...

> **But** God, being rich in mercy, **because of His great love** with which He loved us, even when we were dead in our transgressions, made us alive together with Christ (by grace you have been saved), and raised us up with Him, and seated us with Him in the heavenly places in Christ Jesus.[27]

The simple conjunction "but" rescues us. God is love;[28] He is rich in mercy and He does not desire the death of the wicked.[29]

God desires all men everywhere to be saved.[30] That includes you. Because God is loving, kind, and merciful, He wants to save you from the punishment you deserve.[31]

Tension

There is tremendous tension in this scenario. You are a guilty sinner and God must punish you. But He is also filled with mercy, grace, and lovingkindness, and He desires to forgive you and rescue you. However, if God simply dismissed the cases of guilty criminals, He would not be just. So how can God be just and yet forgiving at the same time? There is one word that breaks that tension: the gospel.

The Gospel

The gospel is as simple as this: you have broken God's laws, but Jesus Christ has paid your fine. Your court case can be dismissed because Jesus Christ has paid your debt to justice. You, a guilty criminal, can go free because the Judge accepts the payment of the death of Jesus Christ on your behalf.

This is why the gospel is called good news. In fact, it is the best news ever. Our biggest problem (facing God on Judgment Day) has been solved. Guilty criminals can have their criminal record expunged, but justice must be satisfied in order for that to happen.

The Bible teaches "without shedding of blood there is no forgiveness" of sins.[32] In order for sins to be forgiven, blood has to be shed—either yours or someone else's.

You could die a thousand deaths and not pay for a single sin because you are a sinful human being. An animal sacrifice cannot pay your debt because sins cannot be forgiven by the sacrifice of a lesser thing. You need a perfect, sinless human representative.

At the same time, because your sins have been committed against God, you also need a divine representative. In other words, you need a God-man to pay for your crimes against God. That is precisely who Jesus Christ is: the God-man who acts as your representative, who is able to offer a divine sacrifice to appease the wrath of God.

Jesus Christ, the Son of God, came to this earth on a rescue mission to seek and save lost people. Jesus Christ, the second Person of the Trinity, took on human flesh, became man, lived a perfect life, and died a brutal death so your sins can be forgiven.

Only the sacrifice of the God-man, Jesus Christ, is sufficient to save you from the wrath of God Himself. Only the death of God the Son can satisfy the wrath of God the Father.

- Jesus had to become a human to represent the human race.

- Jesus had to be God to pay the penalty for your infinitely sinful actions against an infinitely holy God.

Because of His great love, God the Father sent God the Son to pay the penalty for your sins and mine. Jesus Christ received the full fury of God's wrath on the cross so you could be forgiven and set free from the bondage of sin. This was no small price to pay.

Worse Than You Can Imagine

It has rightly been said that death by crucifixion is the most gruesome form of execution ever invented.

- Jesus was stripped naked and mocked by Roman soldiers.

- Jesus was beaten until His face was beyond recognition.

- Jesus' head was smashed by repeated blows from a wooden staff.

- Jesus was whipped with leather straps that had pottery, nails, and broken glass woven in.

- Jesus' hands and feet were pierced by large metal nails.

- Jesus suffocated to death as He hung on a cross.

Look at Jesus, the Diamond of Heaven, beaten to a pulp. See the blood pouring down His shredded body. Hear Him gasp for air as He hangs on a cross with nails piercing His hands and feet. If an eternity in hell sounds horrible, imagine the agony that Jesus experienced when God laid the sin of the world on His Son for everyone who would ever believe.[33]

> For it was the Father's good pleasure for all the fullness to dwell in Him, and through Him to reconcile all things to Himself, having made peace through the blood of His cross; through Him, I say, whether things on earth or things in heaven.
>
> And although you were formerly alienated and hostile in mind, engaged in evil deeds, yet He has now reconciled you in His fleshly body through death, in order to present you before Him holy and blameless and beyond reproach.[34]

The tension is broken. God can now be just and the justifier of those who have sinned against Him.[35] Because of Jesus, God's attributes of mercy and justice can co-exist without compromise. But wait, the good news keeps getting better.

Grace Is Even More Amazing

Through His death, Jesus bore our punishment for the forgiveness of sins, but that act simply brings our sin debt to zero. We still have nothing to commend us to God. We need more than forgiveness; we need righteousness. And Jesus provides that too.

> He made Him who knew no sin to be sin on our behalf, so that we might become the righteousness of God in Him.[36]

Jesus' death on a cross pays your sin debt. His perfect, sinless life grants you righteous standing before God.

Jesus passively surrendered His life, but He actively lived a perfect life for us too. Jesus never sinned; He kept each and every one of God's commandments perfectly and accumulated mountains of righteousness. That goodness gets credited to your account so you can be righteous in the eyes of God.

Instead of being seen as a guilty, shameful criminal, you can be seen as "citizen of the century."

- You give Jesus your rap sheet; He gives you His résumé.

- You give Jesus your badness; Jesus gives you His goodness.

- You give Jesus your massive sin debt; Jesus gives you His infinite righteousness.

Talk about a great exchange! The benefits of the cross are endless.

- God justifies us, declaring us to be "Not guilty."[37]

- God redeems us, buying us out of slavery to sin and the devil.[38]

- God forgives all of our sins—past, present, and future.[39]

- God cleanses us and removes the stain of sin,[40] and makes us righteous.[41]

- God brings us into His family as a beloved child.[42]

- God sanctifies us and gives us His Holy Spirit to empower us to become progressively holy, set apart for His special purposes.[43]

- God grants us eternal life[44] and makes us heirs[45] with an eternal inheritance.[46]

- God declares us saints,[47] prepares a place for us,[48] and allows us to reign with Him forever.[49]

All of that is available to you because of the amazing work of Jesus Christ.

- We celebrate the cure to a disease because Jesus has provided the cure from the disease called sin.

- We love reunion stories because Jesus made it possible for us to be restored to a right relationship with our God.

The One who loves you, the Lord Jesus Christ, accomplished all of this for you. This is the purpose of your existence: to be rescued by King Jesus. You were made by God, for God, to know God, and enjoy God forever. That is why you are here. You are a part of God's cosmic redemption story.

- We love hero stories because Jesus is the greatest Hero ever.

- We love rescue stories because Jesus is the most amazing Rescuer ever.

- We love stories of redemption because Jesus is the greatest Redeemer ever.

Complete forgiveness is available to you right now. All of your sins—past, present, and future—can be forgiven, but a legal transaction must take place. You must have the righteousness of Jesus credited to your account. How does that happen?

> We are made right in God's sight when we trust in Jesus Christ to take away our sins. And we **all can be saved** in this same way, no matter who we are or what we have done. For all have sinned and fall short of God's glorious standard. Yet God now in His **gracious kindness** declares us **not guilty**. He has done this **through Christ Jesus**, who has freed us by taking away our sins. For God sent Jesus to take the punishment for our sins and to satisfy God's anger against us. We are made right with God when we believe that

Jesus shed His blood, sacrificing His life for us.[50]

God Wants to Save You, Not Condemn You

God does not want to send you to hell. God "is patient toward you, not wishing for any to perish but for all to come to repentance."[51] God does indeed send sinners to hell, but that is His peculiar work. God prefers to save sinners, not condemn them.

He will hurtle people to hell because He must, but that is not what He delights in. "Do I have any pleasure in the death of the wicked," declares the Lord GOD, "rather than that he should turn from his ways and live?"[52]

God is a kind God. He is a saving God. He is a loving God. And God is so powerful, He can forgive a sinner like you and transform you into the image of His amazing Son, Jesus Christ.

Your God stands ready to save you. Jesus promises, if you will come to Him on His terms, He will by no means cast you out.[53]

The question is, "What are His terms?"

God's Terms

What must one do to receive the forgiveness (and righteousness) that God freely offers? Guilty criminals do not get to write the terms of their release; God does.

The Bible teaches that you must come to God with correct **knowledge**, correct **motive**, and a correct **response**, or you will not be saved.

1. You must have correct KNOWLEDGE

You must understand God and yourself rightly.[54] What exactly must you understand?

a. God is a triune God (Father, Son, and Holy Spirit) who made the world and everything in it, including you. He owns you.

b. The God-man Jesus Christ was born of a virgin; He kept the laws perfectly and died a horrific death as the sufficient payment for your sins.

c. Jesus rose from the dead and ascended into heaven where He sits at the right hand of the Father.

d. You are sinful by nature and have violated His laws. You justly deserve His temporal and eternal punishment.

e. You can be forgiven and made white as snow because of Jesus' redemptive work.

But mere knowledge is not enough to save you.

2. You must have the right MOTIVE

You should not become a Christian because you desire the benefits of the faith (joy, peace, comfort, everlasting life, etc.). Repent and put your trust in Jesus because He is the source of all good things. If you come seeking the gifts and not the Giver, you will receive neither.

You should not even follow Jesus because you are afraid of hell. You should follow Jesus because He has been so kind to save you from hell. Follow Jesus because He is God and He is good. Very good.

3. You must have the right RESPONSE

The correct response to the shocking news that Jesus saves sinners is: repentance and faith.[55]

Response number one: Repentance

Imagine you and I are in Nebraska in December and we decide to drive to Texas because it is warmer there. I volunteer to drive because I claim to know how to get there. We hop in the car and drive for eight hours when you begin to sense something is wrong.

Your suspicions are confirmed when you see pine trees, snow, and a sign that reads "Canada: 84 miles." We are clearly driving in the wrong direction. What would you like me to do?

1. Upon showing me the evidence of my guilt, you undoubtedly want me to agree with you: you are right, and I am wrong.

2. Of course you don't want me to agree with you and keep heading in the wrong direction; you want me to stop.

3. Now that we are pulled safely off the road, you would like a heartfelt apology.

4. Sitting on the side of the road is not where you want to be, so I suspect you want me to turn around.

5. Now that we are headed in the right direction, you don't want me to just sit there, you want me to start driving to our destination.

6. You want me to keep driving until we get to Texas.

That is true biblical repentance. When someone sins against you, you expect no less than those six things; so does God. This is how Charles Spurgeon defined repentance:

Repentance to be true *must be total*. How many will say, "Lord, I will give up this sin and this other one; but there are certain favorite lusts which I must hang on to." O friends, in God's name let me tell you, it is not the giving up of one sin, nor fifty sins, which is true repentance; it is the serious giving up of every sin.

If you conceal one of these accursed vipers in your heart, then your repentance is nothing but a fake. If you indulge in only one lust, and give up every other, then that one lust, like one leak in a ship, will sink your soul. It is not sufficient just to give up your outward sins; it is not enough just to give up the most wicked sin of your daily life; it is all or nothing which God demands...

All sin must be given up, or else you will never have Christ: all evil must be renounced, or else the gates of heaven must be locked to keep you out forever.

Let us remember, then, that for repentance to be sincere it must be total repentance.[56]

Think of it like this. You come home and enter the front door with your briefcase and a bag of groceries. As your child runs toward you shrieking for joy, you drop your briefcase and groceries in order to put your arms around something much better, your child. That is repentance. You throw down your sins to receive the best thing there is, Jesus Christ.

Repentance is not about perfection; repentance is about heading in a new direction. While you will commit sins as a Christian, you will not sin with joy. You happily give up your sins out of gratitude for the One who died in payment for your sins.

Response number two: Faith

Faith means that you trust Jesus as your Lord and your Savior. You must believe that He is who He says He is, that He truly suffered, died, and rose from the grave.[57] You must put all of your hope in Jesus Christ alone for your salvation.

You must trust Jesus the way you would trust a parachute. If your plane were crashing, you wouldn't merely acknowledge that a parachute could save you; you would put it on. And you must "put on the Lord Jesus Christ"[58] as if your life depends on it. Because it does.

You must deny the existence of any other deity or religious system as if Jesus is the only true and living God who demands exclusive obedience and trust. Because He does.

The Biggest Question

There is only one question remaining, and it is the biggest question you will ever ponder: What will you do with Jesus Christ and His offer of salvation?

Hurry!

When Jesus came to this planet the first time, He was the Lamb of God who was willingly led to the slaughter. The next time He comes, Jesus returns as a warrior. Prepare for a glimpse into the last days on planet earth when meek and mild Jesus goes to war.

> And I saw heaven opened, and behold, a white horse, and He who sat on it is called Faithful and True, and in righteousness He judges and wages war. His eyes are a flame of fire, and on His head are many diadems; and He has a name written on Him which no one knows except Himself. He is clothed with a

robe dipped in blood, and His name is called The Word of God.

And the armies which are in heaven, clothed in fine linen, white and clean, were following Him on white horses. From His mouth comes a sharp sword, so that with it He may strike down the nations, and He will rule them with a rod of iron; and He treads the wine press of the fierce wrath of God, the Almighty. And on His robe and on His thigh He has a name written, "KING OF KINGS, AND LORD OF LORDS."[59]

There is a reason we are so enamored by apocalyptic movies; they are a faint echo of the true apocalypse when Jesus will return, destroy the earth with fire, and judge all nations. It will be a fearsome day.

Then the kings of the earth and the great men and the commanders and the rich and the strong and every slave and free man hid themselves in the caves and among the rocks of the mountains; and they said to the mountains and to the rocks, "Fall on us and hide us from the presence of Him who sits on the throne, and from the wrath of the Lamb; for the great day of their wrath has come, and who is able to stand?"[60]

Nobody can withstand the terrible day of the Lord; and you don't have to.

Jesus said, "Behold, I am coming quickly. Blessed is he who heeds the words of the prophecy of this book."[61] Will you heed this warning? Will Jesus crush you, or will you be hidden in Him and escape that dreadful day? Jesus makes you an offer you truly should not refuse.

Repent and trust in Jesus Christ and He will not go to war with you; He will save you to the uttermost.[62] "Therefore humble yourselves under the mighty hand of God, that He may exalt you at the proper time."[63]

God Will Save Even You

If you think you are beyond God's mercy, you are wrong. God does not save good people; God saves bad people. In fact, He loves to save the dirtiest, most horrific, most despicable kinds of people. If you're one of them, He will save even you.

- Are you a fornicator? Flee to the Savior.

- Are you a pornographer? Then run to Jesus.

- Are you a criminal? Let the Savior cleanse you.

- Are you a drunkard? Fall at the feet of your Redeemer.

The grace of Jesus Christ is beyond comprehension. He is willing to save the worst of the worst. You and I would not save the people that Jesus saves.

- Are you a sexual predator? Jesus died for you.

- Are you a pedophile? He will make you white as snow.

- Are you a woman who aborted your baby? God will grant you mercy.

The worse you are, the more glory He receives for saving a filthy person like you.

Come to him, dirty person, He will make you clean. Do not wait to make yourself clean; you can't. You can do nothing to improve your standing before God. Come as you are. Come now.

> Come you sinner, poor and needy;
> Weak and wounded, sick and sore.
> Jesus, ready, stands to save you;
> Full of pity, love, and power.

Nobody has ever been kinder to you. Your God has created you, fed you, protected you, provided for you, died for you, and now He wants to forgive you.

> As God's partner, **I beg you not to reject this marvelous message of God's great kindness**. For God says, 'At just the right time, I heard you. On the day of salvation, I helped you.' Indeed, God is ready to help you right now. **Today is the day of salvation.**[64]

The King stands ready to pardon. The Judge is willing to dismiss your case. "For God so loved the world, that He gave His only begotten Son, that whoever believes in Him shall not perish, but have eternal life."[65]

- Why would you not want to have your guilt and shame removed?

- Why would you not want to be loved with the greatest love there is?

- Why would you not want your life to make sense and be filled with joy?

This offer is not too good to be true. This offer is true. It is for you. Right now. Today.

Rebel, it is time to repent. It is time to flee to your Creator for mercy. He promises He will not cast you out.

God sets Himself against the proud, but He shows favor to the humble. So humble yourselves before God. Resist the devil, and he will flee from you. Draw close to God, and God will draw close to you. Wash your hands you sinners; purify your hearts you hypocrites. Let there be tears for the wrong you have done. Let there be sorrow and deep grief. Let there be sadness instead of laughter, and gloom instead of joy. When you bow down and admit your dependence on Him, He will lift you up and give you honor.[66]

You could be in a right relationship with the One who demonstrated His love by dying for you...even while you were sinning. Call out to Jesus right now. He is mighty to save.

God will not only forgive you, but He will adopt you as His child and become your heavenly Father. He will love you with the same love He has for His Son, Jesus Christ. You have never known such love.

- Join the masses who have been washed, cleansed, and forgiven.

- Join the multitudes who should be cast into hell but have been given heaven.

- Join the millions who will spend eternity with the King who died for rebels.

Today is the day of salvation. Even now, many are pouring into the Kingdom.

Repent and trust Jesus Christ today... before you stub your toe.

Notes

1. Colossians 1:16
2. Genesis 1:26
3. Psalm 139:1–4
4. Psalm 89:14
5. Romans 2: 16; 2 Corinthians 5:10
6. Hebrews 9:27
7. Exodus 20:3
8. Exodus 20:7
9. Exodus 20:7
10. Exodus 20:12
11. Exodus 20:13
12. Matthew 5:22
13. 1 John 3:15
14. Exodus 20:14
15. Matthew 5:27,28
16. Ecclesiastes 3:11
17. Romans 1:19,20
18. Psalm 19:1–4
19. Romans 2:15
20. Romans 1:18,19
21. Lynne Tuohy, "Ross Video Exploits Notoriety," *Hartford Courant*, May 11, 2005.
22. Jeremiah 17:9
23. James 2:10
24. Hebrews 10:31
25. Matthew 13:42
26. Romans 2:5,6; Jeremiah 7:20
27. Ephesians 2:4–6
28. 1 John 4:8
29. Ezekiel 33:11
30. 1 Timothy 2:4
31. 2 Peter 3:9
32. Hebrews 9:22

33. 1 Peter 2:24
34. Colossians 1:19–22
35. Romans 3:21–26
36. 2 Corinthians 5:21
37. Romans 5:1
38. 1 Peter 1:18,19; Romans 6:17,18
39. Colossians 2:14; 1 John 1:9
40. Hebrews 10:22
41. 2 Corinthians 5:21
42. Romans 8:14–17
43. 1 Corinthians 6:11; 2 Peter 1:3
44. John 11:25,26
45. Romans 8:17
46. 1 Peter 1:3,4
47. Romans 1:7
48. John 14:2,3
49. 2 Timothy 2:12
50. Romans 3:22–26
51. 2 Peter 3:9
52. Ezekiel 18:23
53. John 6:37
54. John 8:23,24
55. Mark 1:15; Acts 20:21
56. C.H. Spurgeon, sermon delivered December 7, 1856, at the Music Hall, Royal Surrey Gardens.
57. 1 Corinthians 15:1–5
58. Romans 13:14
59. Revelation 19:11–16
60. Revelation 6:15–17
61. Revelation 22:7
62. Romans 5:9; Hebrews 7:25
63. 1 Peter 5:6
64. 2 Corinthians 6:1,2
65. John 3:16
66. James 4:6–10

Mindful thoughts for
RUNNERS

First published in the UK in 2019 by

Leaping Hare Press

An imprint of The Quarto Group, The Old Brewery,
6 Blundell Street, London N7 9BH, United Kingdom
T (0)20 7700 6700
www.QuartoKnows.com

British Library Cataloguing-in-Publication Data
A catalogue record for this book is available from the British Library

ISBN: 978-1-78240-764-5

This book was conceived, designed and produced by

Leaping Hare Press

58 West Street, Brighton BN1 2RA, UK

Publisher: *Susan Kelly*
Creative Director: *Michael Whitehead*
Editorial Director: *Tom Kitch*
Art Director: *James Lawrence*
Commissioning Editor: *Monica Perdoni*
Project Editor: *Elizabeth Clinton*
Illustrator: *Lehel Kovacs*

Printed in China

5 7 9 10 8 6 4

Contents

Mindful thoughts for
RUNNERS

Freedom on the trail

Tessa Wardley

Leaping Hare Press

Running
Reimagined

As runners, we all engage with the physicality of running. We understand the ups and downs, the achievements and the failures. We also know that it makes us feel good; it can make us feel more positive, refreshed and ready to take on life's challenges. Approaching running mindfully enables us to use the mental space that running naturally provides. By focusing on the immediate present, and examining our thoughts, emotions and sensations, without judgement, we bring ourselves closer to the subtle and important truths within us. Our own priorities become clear, freed from the distortion of outside influences, the regrets of the past or fears for the future.

Running these days is big business. There is a huge amount of specialized gear available: heart-rate monitors, watches and racks of Lycra. But wherever you are in the world, all you really need is running shoes, and you can lace up, stretch out and explore your new surroundings. You can run on city roads, country lanes, running tracks, up and down mountains, beaches, moorland, on snow, sand, rock or mud – or if none of these are available, you can run on a treadmill. Over the miles, you may begin to learn some new things about yourself and the power of running mindfully.

There are any number of reasons why people run but we are all in search of one thing – that feeling. When a wave of ecstasy breaks over us and we are washed clean of all the clutter of everyday life that clings to our minds. In these moments our bodies and minds work in perfect union, our senses are alive with the pleasure of the moment, the ground flies by, we are light on our feet, everything is bright and vivid. These moments of flow, being in the zone, are the holy grail of all runners.

Mindful running offers an adventure to those who choose to pursue it, a feeling that will feed into all aspects of our lives and nourish the darkest corners of our worlds. Running gives us the opportunity to stay connected with the world and with ourselves.

The purpose of this book is to resonate with your experiences but also to encourage you to pause and think again about your motivations and your expectations – running is so much more than a habit or a form of exercise. A mindful perspective can bring a new depth to your running, a greater awareness of where it can take you and how much you can achieve.

The freedom that running gives us is the ideal opportunity to practise mindful techniques, whether on a day-long cross-country expedition or a quick circuit around the block. Lacing up and heading out mindfully can be a powerful force for wellbeing – more dynamic than just mindfulness, and more rewarding than just running. You may not find flow on every run but in the long term you will certainly reap the rewards.

Finding
Clarity

All runners can tell you tales of runs that kick-started a particularly sluggish morning or turned around feelings of despair and hopelessness at the end of a day that went wrong. When we have had a 'good' run we can face the world with our shoulders firmly back, our head held high and a smile on our faces. The physiological and psychological benefits we can gain from running are such that they resonate throughout the day, altering our outlook and energy, improving our mental acuity and our social interactions, and leading to an impact on every aspect of our lives.

The many physiological benefits of running include improving our cardiovascular health, strengthening our bones and lowering cholesterol. Psychologically, running can reduce stress, improve our self-esteem and result in feelings of positivity. Introducing mindfulness into your running routine will bring further advantages as you set your mind free and focus on the moment, simply putting one foot in front of the other and acknowledging your surroundings as they pass by, finding harmony and serenity in your actions.

PROMOTING CALM

Take the time some day to sit on a bench in a busy park and just watch the runners passing by. Observe the runners who have achieved a steady rhythm. Whatever the diversity in their running styles, you will be amazed at the range of running gaits and rhythms. Look beyond that to their facial expressions, and you will see that their faces invariably radiate focused calm. Master of mindfulness Jon Kabat-Zinn said, 'Running is breath by breath, footstep by footstep, moment by moment . . . It has its own calming and clarifying meditative elements built right in to it'. Running induces this mindful state where we are fully present in the moment, focused on the rhythmic interplay between our footfalls and breath.

Film-makers Matan Rochlitz and Ivo Gormley had noticed the meditative state of the runners in their local park. Investigating further and interviewing runners, they observed the effects of the calming and clarifying nature of running, and found that when they approached the runners they were overwhelmingly relaxed and happy to engage in conversations. Through this openness they were able to discover insights into peoples' lives and hear their stories, both running and wider-life related. Such openness in inner cities is unprecedented – many of us going about our daily business feel as if we are in too much of a rush to respond, reluctant to be distracted while we rush from A to B. Even trying to catch the eye of a stranger on an inner-city bus is a challenge.

Running was providing a moment of mindfulness for these runners. The meditative state was soothing the excess of thoughts that usually crowds in and confuses our thinking; the runners experiencing that clarity of mind were able to access their deep truths. They were able to express their ordered thoughts, and deep insights into their lives were exposed.

One runner who had experienced mental health issues had some advice for fellow sufferers, 'Don't make excuses for the fact that you are feeling bad, don't try to stop yourself from feeling bad, just accept that you are and talk to someone about it.'

Another runner's insight stemmed from the very heart of the mindful approach to life, 'Bear in mind the past and the future but don't ever let them rob you of the present because that is all you've got.'

LIVING IN THE MOMENT

Running is complementary to mindfulness; many runners will be practising mindfulness to some degree through their actions without any conscious attempt to do so. Through the repetitive footfalls and breathing we find it relatively easy to move to a place where body and mind move as one. Absorbed in the action of running, our minds are stilled; we are able to dwell in the present, enjoying the sensations of the body and thus being released from our daily anxieties. This regular release spills over into the rest of the day and further into our lives; when we are in possession of a calmer mind and greater clarity, we can deal better and more intuitively with our day-to-day challenges.

The
Running Bug

Non-runners find runners hard to understand. That constant desire to run wherever and whenever, the itchy twitchiness that comes over the runner when they are unable to lace up and head out for a run for a few days. Like the restorative pleasure of a nice cup of tea to a non-tea drinker, the non-runner cannot understand these emotions and feelings, the gnawing desire that drives someone who has the running bug.

CATCHING THE BUG

Imagine you, as a non-runner, have heard your running friends enthusing about running, how much they love it, how they can't do without it. You like the sound of this wholesome but habit-forming activity so you decide to give it a go. Thinking you will love it, you stride out confidently but don't get very far before you are out of puff; you stop, and then get demoralized. You think 'this is not for me' and you don't go out again for a while. Sometime later you try again, and again you head off too fast and are demoralized when you have to stop. Sometimes that is enough. You conclude running is not for you and label yourself as a non-runner and decide categorically that all runners are crazy.

But sometimes, something else happens. With a bit of persistence or maybe some good advice, you get past that first hurdle. Running is one of the most natural things a human can do; if you get off to the right start, you will soon catch the running bug. Before you know it, you are swinging along. Stride after stride you fall into a rhythm, your breathing falls in line and you realize you can keep it going for longer than you imagined. By the end of the run you are feeling calm and elated. You know you can do it.

RENEWING CONNECTIVITY

Now you have done it once, you want to do it again. You want to feel that sense of achievement, that belief in your body, and more than anything that cool, calm, collected positivity that arises from the meditative rhythm when we run. Living in the moment and focusing on our senses as we run puts us in touch with our bodies and our minds in a way that we had probably forgotten. Our muscles and mind remember how we used to run when we were children. The sad fact is that as we move into adulthood many of us leave behind the connection we once had with our bodies. As we settle down to driving cars, riding on buses and trains and working behind desks, our virtual lives become more real than our living reality. We hem ourselves in to an increasingly restrictive shell of physical caution. Embarking on the activity of running is a fantastic way of renewing the bond between mind and body and the ideal opportunity to use mindful techniques to enrich the experience, to free you from everyday pressures as you focus only on the movement of your body, your breathing and the world around you.

No matter what happens now, you will always know that you have stepped over to the other side – you are now a runner. You understand that hitting your stride and achieving that rhythm will take you to places you had only ever imagined, physically and mentally. You can travel further, experience more and have adventures. You will reach that point where pain and pleasure become one. You know when you set out on a run that you will find pain but you know too that you can keep going; you know the benefits and smooth pleasure you will experience when you have pushed your body hard and achieved your goals. It is not easy, but what in life that is worth doing is easy?

Each run brings its rewards. It does not matter how fast or far you run; we all have our own goals. It is enough that each time we head out, we return with a good feeling about ourselves – the positive outcome of a challenge set and a challenge achieved. Just a few days off will leave us wanting some more; we won't want to take time out, we constantly want more of the calm serenity we find while we are running and the positive feeling and self-confidence it brings.

As a new runner, before long you will find that the positive effects spiral, encompassing everything you do, and running rapidly becomes your life. You are well and truly caught by the running bug.

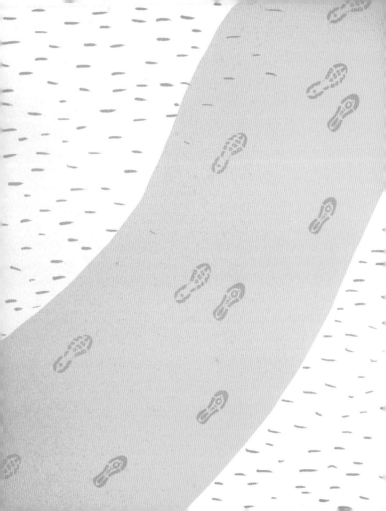

Connecting
with the
Earth

Running is all about our interaction with the earth. We propel ourselves along through the physical exertion of forces on the ground. The speed with which we are able to go depends on the amount of forward propulsion we can extract from the contact between our feet and the ground.

FEET ON THE GROUND

The connection we make with the earth as we run is fundamental to the mindful runner. During the interaction between us and the earth's surface, the sensation of our feet on the ground results in a personal awareness of ourselves in the present. We feel grounded; we are present in our bodies and can feel our bond with the earth and the outside world.

As you run mindfully, be aware of the changing pressures and sensations of the terrain over which you pass. Feel the changing response of the track as you push off – from dry, rutted dirt trails to soft, springy woodland moss or sticky, deep mud which holds your foot as if unwilling to let you pass; hard stones and the edge of paving slabs, tree roots sticking out of the ground and puddles after rain. They all have their own resonance and response to the passage of your feet. Allow the realization of the changes of terrain to connect you and bind you more closely with the present as you revel in the moment. Being aware of this connectivity to the ground beneath your feet makes you more grounded, resulting in a more intense and pleasurable running experience.

GIVE AND TAKE

As we run, we leave our footprints on the earth and in response the earth leaves its impression on us. Touch is a reciprocal exchange with the world. There is a certain knowledge that only feet can enable – there are certain memories of place that only feet can recall. To leave an impression is also to receive one. As the soles of our feet leave an impression, so a reciprocal impression is left in our consciousness – we are left with a physical knowledge of the place that we have passed through and a memory is imprinted in our minds.

Sensing the changes in texture and pressure working on our feet also works on our mind, altering the textures and inclinations of our thoughts. When we have run through a location the resultant memories and recollections of that place will be much altered from those that develop if we have cycled or driven that way before. Running through the landscape brings us into direct contact with the world, something that other modes of transport cannot replicate. The physical

connection with the air and the ground, the immediacy
of sights, sounds and smells allows us to vividly recall
those surroundings.

BAREFOOT RUNNING

There is an increasing trend amongst runners to run
barefoot, enjoying an even closer connection to the
earth. Losing the shoes is like shedding a skin. You find
yourself at the same time more vulnerable and more
sensitive to all the earth has to offer. Running barefoot,
you become aware of previously unsensed subtle changes
in temperature and texture as you run over patches of
sunlight on the trail, damp and dry soil or vegetation.
You will know within a split second when you pass a
spiky-leaved plant. As you expose yourself to the trail
you feel so much more – every sensation is amplified;
the connection to your surroundings has increased in its
intensity. You are fully alive in the moment, all senses
firing. Running barefoot causes you to become more
attentive to your own time and place.

Barefoot runners claim to be happier and more injury-free without their shoes, but just bear in mind that it can take weeks and months to build up your foot strength and harden the skin on your feet necessary for faster or longer runs, and running on some terrain will always be a challenge with no shoes at all.

All forms of running create a connection between us and the earth and remind us of our responsibilities to our world. As you run, meditate on your footprint, think about your connection to the world and consider ways in which you can lighten your impact and reduce your carbon footprint. Re-using water bottles, choosing sustainable and fair-trade food and fabrics – as runners we can play our part. We owe it to ourselves and our futures to tread lightly and mindfully on the earth.

The Call
of the
Wild

We all come from the wild; it resides, embedded, in all of us. Listen to its call and take a step into nature to reignite that connection, see the world with a new perspective and nourish your soul.

RECONNECT WITH THE WORLD

There is a certain soft focus that we can achieve through mindful running that allows us to see the world in a slightly different way. By letting go of the narrow focus of our minds we take in the world through a slightly wider perspective, one that does not just see the brightest lights and the loudest sounds that usually draw all our attention. With this wider perspective, borne of mindfulness, a runner becomes aware of the silence between sounds and the shadows between shapes – the negative spaces in the world.

But it is not just the detail of the world that we see differently. As runners, we see the landscape in all its dimensions, with all its beauty and wonder but also all its opportunities. When we look out over the land we see not only the majesty of hills and dales, the form, colour and texture of rivers, woodlands and rock, but we also see routes to be run, a landscape to get into and be part of: riverbanks that lead to rocky paths, and rocky paths climbing to ridges that will lift the soul, peaks that link to other peaks, valleys to swoop down and lakes to soak our feet in at the end of a gnarly trail.

It's easy to feel cut off from the natural world when we spend so much of our day in cars and buildings, looking at screens and communicating virtually. To go for a run in nature is to reconnect to our former selves.

Just a few steps in you are instantly aware of the season. The scream of the new season's birds as they fly high, performing dramatic loop-the-loops as they catch insects on the wing, back from their long migration. There are countless small signs that signify our place in the year and link us to the seasons. Sitting inside an artificially lit room, we can be surprised to find we have lost track of the time of day. Many's the time I've togged up and headed out only to discover the day is almost done. Reconnecting with the natural world is reassuring and calms the soul. The knowledge that deep down the earth is still turning, the seasons are changing and all is well with the world – this provides security and helps to put into perspective our own often minor aggravations and inconveniences that grow to dominate our lives.

CHANGE THE ROUTINE

Any run in the natural world is a joy but the best runs are those when you slightly break the mould. Maybe you head out at an unusual time of day, go a bit further than usual, run in bad weather that most would avoid or head off the beaten path. That little bit of extra effort in these runs is often rewarded by an unexpected encounter with the wild: a view from a new angle suddenly changing your perspective on a regular scene, or the brilliant, biblical light of sun through storm clouds – the apocryphal cloud with a silver lining. Some of my best experiences have been with wild animals surprised by my relatively rapid and silent arrival: the memory of coming face to face with a golden eagle as I turned the corner on a mountain run can still lift my mood whenever I recall it – even ten years on. The black depths of its eye and cruelly curved beak, surveying me impassively from metres away before launching off its rock, wings wide enough to fill the sky, the down-draught lifting the dust in swirls around my head. The fact that we can even momentarily share these animals' space is a privilege; that these experiences are spontaneous and entirely beyond our control is at once humbling and invigorating.

Let the wild world call you to it – connect with your world and open up a lifetime of opportunity and adventure. Moments such as these are precious and privileged. They give us a profound feeling of connectedness with our world and provide great perspective to our everyday lives. The power and immensity of the nature that we encounter reminds us of our insignificance in the grander scheme of things, and our humility and wonder at the world reminds us of the responsibility we have to our wild places and the value they have for our future health and prosperity.

The
Ups & Downs
of Running

Out on a run you reach a parting of the ways. One way heads off along a gentle, flat path winding its way out of sight with no ups and no downs. The other path can be seen heading straight up, over the hills into the distance. Which path do you take?

TAKE UP THE CHALLENGE

Let us say for the sake of argument that you choose to take the easy option: the flat path. You can run at the same pace for miles, and nothing gets in your way. Well that's fine for today, maybe it's a day when you don't feel up to a challenge, but what about the next day and the day after that? If we always stay on the flat path we miss out on half of the world, we don't get stronger, we never get the view from the top of the hill and we never get the sweet relief of running down the other side.

The other option is to take what initially seemed the harder, hilly path. It is arduous work. Within minutes you are sweating and puffing your way up the side of the hill; you may even need to walk a bit, but eventually you reach the top – and you have an immense sense of achievement, you can see for miles, and the shallow downhill path winding into the valley looks so inviting you just can't wait to get on it. And more than anything, you know that you can make it the next time you face the challenge.

Running in the hills is all about relativity. When we approach the choice between taking the flat or hilly option we are considering the relative sensations of hard running uphill as compared to the ease of running on the flat. It is the realization of the contrasts in these sensations that can make one feel significantly better than the other. The sensation of discomfort in running up the hill can only be explained when considered in relation to the relative speed and ease of running downhill. It is only through the dark that we enjoy the light, and through pain that we notice pleasure; without the contrast, we would have no means to compare or express the counter sensation.

GROWING STRONGER

The ups and downs we face in running compare exactly to the ups and downs in life and we can learn to approach them in much the same way. Hills in running are like challenges in life. While it can be tempting to detour around life's challenges, this is only a short-term solution.

If we avoid life's challenges then we stagnate; we never grow and we never progress. The challenges may be scary and hard work but they will stretch us, make us use our strengths and develop our skills. These are the things that build our self-esteem and give us confidence to take on more challenges and see more of the world and the variety and beauty of life within it.

A mindful approach can help us to achieve and appreciate the ups. As you start to rise up the hill, concentrate on the here and now – don't focus on the goal, enjoy the journey. Focusing your eyes on a point a few metres ahead and focusing your mind on your breathing aids concentration; all that matters is within you. The pleasure of using our body, to feel every muscle and sinew straining and the lungs burning is to really, truly feel alive.

Remember though that when we take on a hill or challenge, there is folly in thinking that once it is achieved, we can stop there. There will always be the next hill and the next challenge. Reaching the brow of one hill is an achievement but it is not an end in itself. One hill inevitably leads to another, each one furthering our view of the world and ourselves, and taking us forward in our personal development – but don't expect its achievement to be the end.

We should embrace the hills in running and the challenges in life; they are inevitable and they make us stronger; they provide opportunities for pleasure and contrast. To resist is counter-productive because it will simply feel harder the next time.

The Power of
Breath

Breathing is one of the most powerful tools at our disposal in maintaining our emotional and physical balance in life, but so often we waste its potential. We all breathe constantly but the capacity to harness the resulting energy is often lost as we inhale and exhale shallow breaths, only utilizing the very top section of our lungs rather than breathing into every corner.

MAXIMIZING POTENTIAL

Being aware of our breathing and maximizing its possibilities can have a huge impact on our general wellbeing. When we control our breathing, we can support our nervous systems and control our emotional state. Anxiety, poor sleep and stress can all be improved by 'good' breathing. Improving these aspects of our lives creates a positive cycle of health benefits which multiplies, having implications throughout all aspects of our wellbeing.

The rhythm that we find breathing deeply and evenly, breath after breath, provides an important meditative focus as we run too, as well as a metronomic beat on which to build our cadence and stride. This strong rhythm is the basis of our mindful running and is one of the reasons that running lends itself so naturally to mindfulness practice.

BREATHING PROBLEMS

Many factors can throw your breathing out of balance, and one of the worst culprits can be other runners. We've all experienced the heavy breather coming up behind, disrupting our rhythm, throwing us into a breathing crisis. If this happens make sure to focus back on your own breathing – leave behind what is going on with other runners, link your footfall with your own breathing and regain your rhythm.

Fatigue can also play its part. As the run progresses and you start to struggle, the mind begins to wander and unhelpful thoughts start to surface. How far is it to the end? Why are people going past me? Is the wind getting stronger? I'm too hot. The mind can throw up any number of barriers to success; bringing the focus back to your breathing can be a race saver.

BREATHING CORRECTLY

Before you start to run, it can be useful to begin by priming your breathing. Take a few deep breaths, in through the nose and out through the mouth. These can be quite forceful. Focus in on the sensation of the breaths. Notice how the body expands with the in-breath, the sensation of the chest rising and air filling the lungs, nourishing you, strengthening you and feeding your body. To maximize the volume of air you can breathe, remember to keep your neck and spine long, your chest open and breathe right down into your belly. As you breathe in, feel the air rush in and nourish you; as you breathe out, feel the air around you and notice how your body relaxes and softens. Doing this before you start to run can help to fix the sensations of this relaxation and softening of the body; as you run this physical memory is carried with you, to be recalled in moments of need.

As you run, build the rhythm between your footsteps and your breathing – let the body follow the breath and the breath follow the body. Focus on enjoying the awareness of space around you and the feel of the breeze on your skin and in your hair. Settle into that natural rhythm of breathing and footfalls. Your mind may wander and thoughts will come and go. If these thoughts are becoming unhelpful then bring the focus back to the breath and the footfalls – deep and even. Feel your body fill on the inhale, and feel the relaxation as you breathe out and expel the negative thoughts.

Sometimes when a run gets really hard, a gentle focus is not enough; intensify your focus by counting your footsteps while maintaining your breathing rhythm. Count every right foot strike in sets of ten, twenty, fifty – whichever seems to suit the moment best. You can even count in twos – one two, one two, one two. This breaks the exercise down and helps you to focus in on the now, removing anxiety and carrying you through a tough phase. Being comfortable with this style of rhythmic breathing reduces the chances of an injury by improving balance and reducing tension in your body. Increased body balance will enable you to incorporate different surfaces and different speeds more easily. With the greater awareness of your surroundings, borne of mindful breathing and relaxation, you can, quite literally, take everything in your stride.

So don't just take breathing for granted. By employing mindful breathing as we run we can restore our energy, maximize our oxygen supply, relax our bodies and our mind and help improve our long-term wellbeing.

Enjoying
the Elements

It is ingrained in us from an early age that we should try to combat the elements, keep them out, perhaps even stay indoors when it's wet or cold. As the author Alfred Wainwright noted, 'There's no such thing as bad weather, only unsuitable clothing'. This is very relevant to the runner, for whom extreme weather conditions can present a challenge. The heat of the sun, heavy rain, wind, ice and snow – they all provide their own hardships, but very often all that is needed to keep us safe is the right clothing.

COME RAIN OR SHINE

More important when dealing with the elements is our state of mind. How we perceive the weather is only partly dictated by the conditions but is strongly influenced by how we are feeling, and we can change this by using mindful techniques. Imagine yourself heading out on a run; it's a beautiful sunny day with a cooling breeze. The world feels alive and bright, the greenery is radiant, the hills are sharp against the horizon, the sunlight is glinting playfully off the surface of the water and the refreshing wind is whispering in the long grass. As you run you start to get tired; before you know it you are focusing on the heat, it feels overpowering, the wind is blowing against you and the glare of the sun off the surface of the water is blinding. Nothing has changed in the weather; your unhelpful thoughts are taking over and a negative perception of the elements is developing.

By employing a little mindfulness we can change our frame of mind and our mental approach to facing the elements. We can return that unremitting glare and searing heat back to bright sunlight and brilliant views.

It seems we rarely allow ourselves to accept the weather, to enjoy just being present in what the world has given us today. We fight and rail against the conditions. We can be so negative that sometimes we can't even enjoy the present for fear of what may be around the corner. Some people are never happy – too icy, too hot, too wet, too windy and even when the weather appears to be perfect, 'Well I don't suppose it will last'. We delight in our elemental battles.

CHANGING ATTITUDES

Ultimately we need to accept the weather as it is. We may not particularly like being wet or cold and so we can take physical interventions to insulate ourselves from the worst of it. The important difference is the spirit with which we approach facing the elements: do we grit our teeth and fight our way against the wind and rain, shoulders tight and head down?

Accepting the weather and heading out, appropriately attired, with a positive attitude, we may find there is more pleasure to be gained than we expected. When we live in the moment we can challenge the negative thinking and feel liberated and exhilarated. One moment the wind in your face may be hard to battle against and the rain is a strength-sapping drenching. At these moments focus on maintaining your form, accept the slower pace but keep moving. Seeing it as a battle is never going to work; fighting the wind will not make it stop blowing. However, at some point you will turn a corner and suddenly the wind is your friend – like a hand in the small of your back the wind urges you onwards, encouraging you towards your goal, and as you warm up the rain becomes refreshing, a pleasantly cooling drizzle.

Sometimes the combination of the elements can be so bad as to be laughable – freezing rain with horizontal winds driving it into your face like shards of glass, making forward motion almost impossible.

The great opportunity in running is that by getting out in all weathers, we are truly immersed and involved, and we are really living with nature. Once you accept the elements, running in the rain can leave a buzz in your soul that raises the spirits for hours – you can release your tensions to the four winds, which seem to blow them away and lighten your soul, leaving you giddy and light-headed. The physics of the element is objective, but how we deal with it is subjective. By living in the present and freeing ourselves from elemental preconceptions, we can change our view of the rain, snow, heat and wind, and head out in excitement.

A Meditation on
Freedom

Freedom can be hard to define. It is one of
our most basic human needs and even
rights. We deny people their freedom
as a punishment and many people
have died in the pursuit of freedom
from oppressive regimes and
ideologies. It can be hard to define
but we all know how we feel when
we don't have it and we recognize it
when we experience it.

BREAKING AWAY

We can all feel physically and mentally constrained by life at times. The need to dress and behave in a certain way, to move at a steady pace amongst our fellow human beings, to follow certain routines, to turn up to work, to look after our families and loved ones, to respond to emails, phone calls, social media – whatever dictates our daily lives, at times all these obligations can feel oppressive and restrictive, taking up every waking minute of our day.

Running represents freedom. Freedom from others and freedom from ourselves; the freedom to partake in aimless movement, to just get out the door and away from our responsibilities.

FREE YOUR BODY AND YOUR MIND

As we get older we tend to run less and less. We don't use our bodies the way we did as children; we become more sedentary, move more slowly, become more physically cautious. Running liberates us physically from the static immobility that creeps up on us unnoticed. There are other benefits too, in the amount of ground we can cover.

Heading out on a run is one of the most simple activities but demonstrates our freedom to us – next time you are feeling constrained, just head out the door and run. In our work clothes, a two-minute run is a little adventure, an escapade that brightens our lives and takes us out of the mundane. Knowing we have that freedom in our lives is sometimes enough. Just the knowledge that it exists can allow us to relax and enjoy the rest of our time, taking on what previously felt like burdens but facing them as an enjoyable challenge.

We can practise mindfulness on the shortest of runs, but on a longer run we can find profound mental freedom. Our minds can get so clogged up and cluttered that it can be hard to see the way forwards. Running mindfully provides an opportunity to find freedom from the mental clamour. As you get into your rhythm let your mind run free; don't try to control it, just allow the thoughts to come and go. At first as you run there will be a scramble for attention – thoughts will ping in and out of your mind, vying for the top spot in the anxiety rankings. Don't beat yourself up about it; just keep running. Step by step, breath by breath. Notice how the thoughts slow down, and become less insistent. Observe your breathing and how your stride feels strong. Now you can hardly even notice your thoughts; you are fully focused on enjoying the run. Feelings of calm and elation wash over you as you swing along, absorbed in the rhythm of the movement. As we run and reach into our meditative state, our mind calms and the ripples smooth.

As you emerge from your running state, you start to be aware of your thoughts and previous anxieties but they seem less insistent than before, less of a clamour and a clutter. You can see a way through the challenges; they seem more manageable. You have enjoyed a bit of freedom from the overactivity of your mental burden and now you can reap the rewards.

When we lace up our running shoes and head out the door we are exercising our right to be free. It is partly an escape from the pressures of life, it is partly an escape from ourselves, but it is more than that; it is proof that one of the simplest activities we can perform, putting one foot in front of the other over and over again, can make us feel free as we challenge ourselves and succeed. The knowledge and promise of such freedom sustains us.

Creative
Running

We all contain creative energy. We may not be artists or musicians but we all have the capacity for creative thought and problem solving. Whatever your creative outlet, sometimes the route to accessing it is blocked, and like water in a river dammed by fallen branches our creative energy cannot find its outlet. There are many reasons why this blockage forms – the noise of life can fill our minds, or the rules, regulations and processes set out for us to follow stifle our creativity. Sometimes we are trying too hard to find an answer, or maybe we just don't believe we have that creative ability within us and we have no idea it is there.

Running is a wonderful vehicle to help you to release your creative energy. As you run, you reach a point where you are running with a rhythm and ease that allow the miles to fly by. In this state, also known as the state of flow, the mind is calmed enough that our unconscious mind is given some space to work. The barriers are broken down and our creativity is released.

RELEASE THE FLOW

We can access our innate and spontaneous intelligence by using it without forcing it. Like dammed-up water released in a rush, our ideas can be turbulent and unfocused at first. But as we run with them they begin to take some order, as our mind sifts them and retrieves the best solutions. Our creative mind is at work, forming new ideas and making new linkages. Creative solutions, works of art, paragraphs of writing all have space to float to the surface. Order reigns as the thoughts flow freely, smoothly connecting new ideas with sense and logic.

In this state of flow, the unthinkable ingenuity and creative power of our spontaneous and natural functioning, which may be blocked when we try too hard to master something by formal methods and techniques, is released.

ESCAPING INTELLECTUAL THOUGHT

The occasions when we really feel ourselves flying happen when we approach the run with a certain sense of 'non-graspingness of mind', an idea which is often referred to in mindfulness literature. This state of mind can be a hard concept to understand. It relates to the fact that our mind likes to think it is in control. Our intellect likes to battle with understanding the world around us, categorizing and boxing everything off – but the world is more complex than that and we cannot hope to understand, classify and control everything, so our brain goes into a spin. If, however, we can turn off our intellect, just for a short while, then we can release all sorts of unknown energy and make linkages that were previously unavailable to us. We can reach clarity and decisions spontaneously. It's a bit like allowing the eyes to relax into long-distance vision. Try looking at an object in the foreground, then relax the eyes for long-distance vision. We are still able to see the object near to us but we can now see it in its wider context at the same time.

Some of the world's most creative thinkers have used running as a tool, not least Alan Turing, the creative mind behind artificial intelligence and modern computing. Alan Turing ran great distances, and fast – his marathon time of two hours, forty-six minutes in 1947 would have placed him fifteenth in the Olympic Games the following year. Modern artists who have been inspired by their running include writers Haruki Murakami, Joyce Carol Oates and Malcolm Gladwell and many marathon-running musicians from P. Diddy to Alanis Morissette. At the first International Festival of Running the audience drew people from all walks of life: philosophers, anthropologists, performance artists, graphic designers, cultural geographers, academics and teachers, music and meditation experts – but all of them runners.

When we relax our mental control, our minds are not only able to understand what we already know but can access new resources. We are able to be more receptive to new ideas and concepts – nothing is rejected, and we are fully open to the opportunities of new knowledge and a new understanding. Creativity can flow.

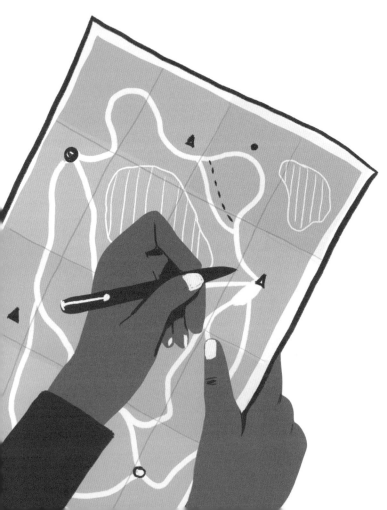

The Road
Less Travelled

The repetitive rhythms of running provide a great opportunity for mindfulness, but relying on recurring actions can become a way of life that impinges on our running. It is easy to get stuck in a running rut. Without thinking we head out of the door, and without employing our brains our feet take us on the same set of routes; day after day, week after week, we run the same handful of paths and trails.

EXPLORE THE UNKNOWN

In this act of mindlessness we are depriving ourselves of a great opportunity – the opportunity to explore. Mindfulness has within it an innate sense of curiosity.

When we live in the moment we are always aware of what is going on in our present; we are alive to ourselves but also to our surroundings. We notice the side paths and wonder where they will take us. We are stimulated to wonder at the world, to find out what is going on just out of view. We are drawn in to life.

Running takes us out into our local environment and provides the perfect opportunity to explore the road less travelled, to inject a bit of the unknown into our lives. So why not employ a sense of adventure and curiosity? Find somewhere new to visit, new paths to travel and a new view to see. Planning can start before we even leave the house. Have a map ready at home; put it on the wall, and look out for previously unvisited areas, or paths you have never noticed. Just a short section of path previously unrun can show us the familiar in a different way; we can find gems of open country in the most grey suburban sprawl, pockets of undiscovered beauty in an area we thought we knew, igniting our interest and allowing us to wonder at our world.

If you travel for work, pack your running shoes. Even in a seemingly uninspiring concrete jungle, by following the road less travelled you can find uplifting moments: areas of parkland, waterside paths, historic cobbled streets. The unexpected and inspiring is around every corner – it can lift the prospect of a mundane working day to unexpected heights.

KEEP MOTIVATED

The danger of constantly rerunning just the same handful of routes at the same time of day is that we develop a narrow focus. With little to interest us in our surroundings there is little chance of new experiences and the focus is inevitably drawn in closer to ourselves. Our chance of success in this situation is restricted to our personal performance. Allowing this very restricting view of running means that if our performance drops or reaches a plateau, then we are in danger of losing our motivation to run. When we are less motivated we find reasons not to run, our successes become less frequent and a downward spiral begins, with less running, less fun and less success.

By maintaining our mindful focus as we run, we are present in our surroundings as well as in ourselves. We are drawn into new areas; new observations and new experiences keep our running alive. If we can maintain our interest in running then there will be more opportunities for success and there will always be one positive element to draw us out the door. The more fun we are having, the more we want to keep running; the more we run, the more success we have, and the positive spiral grows.

Taking the road less travelled is not just about taking different paths; it can simply mean doing things in a slightly different way. It may be as simple as changing your routines – running at a different time of day, with different people, on your own or in conditions you would normally avoid. Try not to limit yourself just because you have always done something one way; challenge your thinking. American landscape designer

John Brinckerhoff Jackson said, 'The road offered a journey into the unknown that could end up allowing us to discover who we were'. By taking that step onto the road less travelled we may end up doing just that.

On every run we can learn something new – about our environment, ourselves and our place in the world. Our inner landscapes are powerfully shaped by our mindful experience of the outer landscape. Allow yourself to wonder at the world, keep your running alive and curious, and you will enjoy your running more and want to head out more often – these are the rewards of the road less travelled.

Pace
Yourself

From a young age, we learn from the fable of the tortoise and the hare that it is important to balance the desire to start off at a fast pace with an understanding of the best way to manage the long race ahead.

As the hare soon learned, starting off fast will not always mean you are first to the finishing line. Pacing yourself means that you may need to hold yourself back, slow down or stop before you want to. That can be a challenge, but experience shows us that if we pace ourselves we will have fewer periods when we crash and burn and then we can achieve much more. Getting the pace wrong is one of the most common mistakes made by runners at all levels. 'I went out too fast', or 'I had nothing left at the end' – you are as likely to hear these cries of despair at an Olympic post-race interview as you are at your local running club. It seems we find it hard to pace ourselves.

A significant pace risk factor is allowing ourselves to focus too closely on others. If we see other runners heading off at a fast pace, we worry about being left behind. We respond by trying to run faster than we should. But we know ourselves best. The balance of available energy and the demands on it are specific to you so try not to look to others for guidance; look inside yourself. Like the tortoise, we know our own running pace. Through mindful awareness, we can pay attention to the stimuli that we allow in, and have the confidence to stick to the pace that suits us best.

CONSERVING ENERGY

Our energy is a limited resource. With the self-awareness born of mindfulness we can also interpret our energy levels effectively. We can learn to balance our energy levels with the demands we anticipate on our path. In running, as in life, this means balancing periods of activity with periods of rest. Our energy is a precious commodity; we need to guard it carefully. Mindful self-awareness can help you pace your running to your own energy levels so that you can do more of it and achieve your goals.

There are certain behaviours that can tempt us away from an effective pace; one of these is being on autopilot. On autopilot we tend to rush things to get them done, but rushing rarely gets anything done to the standards that we expect of ourselves – so we end up frustrated and disappointed. In our running this means failing to achieve times and sometimes not even completing the distance. Bringing a mindful awareness to our running interrupts that mindless autopilot behaviour and with it the tendency to rush. Instead, we are present in the moment; we observe our energy levels and are therefore able to remind ourselves to take things steadily, and run at the pace that suits us best.

GETTING TO THE FINISH LINE

In running we are often encouraged to 'leave it all on the track'. The aim is that at the end of the run you have used up all your resources, your heart and soul and every last ounce of energy, to achieve your goal – but this needs to be timed to perfection. Using up all your energy in the first few hundred metres is not going to achieve that goal. Many is the race when I have headed out powerfully and full of optimism and ended the race ragged, being passed by others as I dragged myself forwards. For years runners tried to head out hard and hang on to complete races in world-beating times, but it never worked. Eventually, through many tough lessons, running wisdom showed that the most effective way to achieve a certain time was always to aim for an even pace.

The wisdom of experienced runners suggests that we should learn not to race at the beginning of a run but to stay present with ourselves, avoid going on autopilot and not focus on the runners around us. The mental boost when you pass other competitors in the second half of a gruelling race is immense, particularly in contrast to the mental demoralization of being passed by waves of runners yourself.

Learning your pace is an important lesson in life. Slow down and be deliberate in your actions. Don't just go at running or life unthinkingly with unfocused passion. Instead, learn to be present and develop your self-awareness; balance your energy inputs and outputs to achieve the best outcomes. Making deliberate choices in the present can save a lot of the anxiety and regrets that can occur in the future when you are wiped out and exhausted before you even reach your goal.

The
Long Run

Setting out on a long run can give you a great feeling, when you know that your body is ready for it, it's a nice day, the path is reaching out in front of you and time is on your side. The long run provides that opportunity to really step outside of ourselves and our daily lives, to push it all to the side and just settle in to our stride. The simplicity of the long run is beautiful, footstep after footstep, breath after breath, but it can also present some particular challenges as the body becomes tired. These can be overcome with the use of mindful techniques, helping you reach your goal without exhausting yourself.

Space and the opportunity to spend time with yourself are rare commodities these days and both have long-term benefits for our mental health. Rather than being dominated by the thoughts and opinions of others, we get the time and space to see how our own minds work, to find out how we are getting on, to develop our own views on the world and how it is treating us. But is that what is actually going on in our minds as we run?

What goes on in the mind of the runner is a great mystery to those who don't run. We are often asked what we think about, out there, all day, running. Most runners will find this question difficult to answer. Aside from the first few minutes of any run, most runners will say, when pushed, that ultimately they run in a bit of a mental void; thoughts drift into the mind like clouds drifting across a clear sky, barely coming into focus as they move in and out, making little impact, leaving little more behind them than a residual breeze. Some runners will see this as a state of Zen, the ultimate in mindfulness; others will see it as a state of survival.

KEEP POSITIVE

Once your body settles into the rhythm of the run you will have periods when you feel as if the day and the path could be endless. That there is no reason why you should not just keep going until you run out of land. But then arrives the time that appears on every long run when the mind or the body rebels. Doubts and anxieties start to build up, and negative thoughts begin to arise. Why am I doing this? Can I really run all the way? My feet are aching – maybe I'll just stop and walk for a while.

Now is the time to employ some mindfulness practice. Turn your attention to your breathing to help you to regain your rhythm; as your breathing comes under control, move on to your form, keep your knees facing forwards and your feet light on the ground. Your body will feel lighter and less of a burden. Don't allow the negative thoughts to spiral out of control; acknowledge them and allow them to move on. Before long you will regain your composure and will be swinging along again, back in balance.

STRIKING OUT

As you run mindfully, look around you and enjoy your location, expand your observations beyond your inner focus – one of the pleasures of the long run is the opportunity to cover more ground. By covering greater distances we can observe more than just our local environment. It is an opportunity to experience more of the area that we live in or even to travel further afield and expand our horizons in a new area.

Another visceral joy of a long run is the effect on the body. A large part of the day spent out in the open air leaves a deep hunger and fatigue that just has to be answered. Food will never taste better and any bed will do. The additionally intense sense of personal achievement that goes alongside the physical and mental benefits is the icing on the cake. It builds self-confidence and makes you stand tall. The day after a long run, when the body aches and the soul is happy, there resides a deep state of calm, satisfaction and self-awareness, an inner knowledge that is shared by all those who are long-distance runners and unknowable to those who are not.

Listen
to Your Body

Running can be a wonderful vehicle towards increased mindfulness; the naturally meditative action can help us to live in the moment more readily and more directly than we can in other settings. Achieving a greater mindfulness as we move can also help us as runners.

RECOGNIZE THE SIGNS

Running is a balance between pushing ourselves to our physical limits and being mindful not to push ourselves beyond those limits. Every runner dreads injury and having to take time off from running. It is therefore important for runners to have an awareness of their bodies and when they are struggling. As we train we learn how to push ourselves but we also need to learn when we are exceeding safe limits and to respond accordingly. It is a fine line but the implications of overtraining and pushing ourselves too far are injuries and illness, which lead to enforced downtime.

THE FULL BODY SCAN

A preventative tool is the full body scan, which centres us in our physical being and brings us into the present moment. Carrying out this exercise as we run is a useful way to bring us into full awareness not only of the moment but also of ourselves. We can review how we are getting on – areas of physical niggles and the sensations of running. In this way we can identify problems before they develop.

As you are running and get into your stride, take a moment to focus on each part of your body in turn. Make a note of how it feels, the pulse and flow of tension and relaxation as your body moves. Being aware of your body when you are relaxed and in a rhythm provides a baseline for comparison with how your body feels when things start to get tougher. Periodically throughout your run revisit this body-scanning process – recognize how your body reacts to the different phases of the run and learn how it responds to the physical stress as it develops.

As your fitness increases you will be aware of how your body changes; you will notice the good days and the bad days. With this kind of full-body mindfulness you will be able to recognize those days when your body is struggling – maybe you have a virus or you are tired – and you will learn that you can be kind to yourself on those occasions and ease off. Better to ease off and return to a tougher session the next time than to push hard and risk having to take extended time off.

THE POST-RUN DEBRIEF

Maintaining your mindfulness at the end of the run is another opportunity to retain that awareness of your body and mind. You could carry out a physical and mental debrief as you warm down and stretch: how did the run pan out? How did the aches and pains respond? Were you able to keep going when you felt like stopping? Are there any indications that you should have stopped or that you have pushed too far?

By listening to our bodies and maintaining mindful contact with ourselves, we learn how to get the best from our bodies, when to stop and when to push on. Running is low on technical equipment; all we have is our bodies and our minds, and we need to bring them into unison and learn to treat what we have well.

Employing mindfulness on every run will provide a little more depth and clarity to your personal understanding. Throughout our lives we develop physical and psychological boundaries, and our perception of these boundaries can be transformed with a mindful approach to running. You learn your limits, when you can push yourself and when you need to stop, to accept that enough is enough. These are important lessons to learn, in life as well as in running. We all have our own rhythm and we all have our own limits – better to set those limits for yourself through a deep understanding of yourself than be told where to put them by someone else or be forced to stop by the immovable barrier of physical injury. When we look mindfully into ourselves and what we are capable of, we are sometimes surprised by what we find; we can often prove ourself to be stronger and endure much more than we ever supposed.

Dealing with
Injury

In spite of all our efforts to maintain balance in our lives through our mindfulness and running practices, there will be times when illness and injury take hold and we cannot run. As runners we often feel that our physical wellbeing is strongly linked to our emotional wellbeing, so how do we cope with managing our emotional wellbeing during the inevitable downtimes of injuries and illness?

Running can become such an important part of our lives that it can feel like the glue that holds everything together. We use running as a tool to build our physical and emotional resilience; it can also be the basis of our social network and our sense of community. Running can become so entwined with our sense of self that we can feel that we are losing ourselves when we are not able to do it. Having it taken away from us, even temporarily, can make us feel anxious and exposed, uncertain about our ability to cope with the rest of our lives.

ACKNOWLEDGE AND ACCEPT

While having to stop running may feel like a backward step in our journey, it does not have to be. Practising mindfulness when we are facing recovery and rehabilitation will be a great support to us as it can help us to achieve the first two stages necessary in any recovery – those of acknowledgement and acceptance. Mindfulness can help us to acknowledge the emotional fear and the physical pain associated with the injury. Through this process we do not allow the pain to take over our whole being but neither do we try to block it out and pretend it is not there. When we acknowledge the pain and live with it then we remove some of its power, and the balance tips in our favour.

Once an injury has arisen and we need to stop running, the situation is out of our control and we must learn to accept it. If we fail to accept the diagnosis and try to keep running through it, we risk making the injury worse. As we resist an injury, we tend to increase our anxiety, which is not a conducive environment for healing. From a position of acceptance we set up a more positive environment, providing our bodies with the best chance of a speedy recovery.

Through acknowledgement and acceptance, we can maintain an emotional balance. We relax into the pain, releasing our anxiety over it. As we face the pain, mindfulness encourages us to focus on our whole body, those parts that are feeling fine as well as those parts that are suffering. We are then encouraged to focus and allow our minds to sink into the pain, breathing naturally and living with the sensation. Injuries need time to heal; allowing our bodies this kind of positive, accepting space encourages the healing process and decreases our anxiety throughout.

THINKING POSITIVELY

If we can learn to accept our injury and reduce our anxiety then we may even find a positive outcome from the adversity. Living in the moment throughout mindfulness practice will allow us to notice that we are still OK. We discover that we can keep living without running. We may even discover that life without running can still be fun. It is possible to maintain our balance and be happy in a less than perfect situation; we can make plans and have expectations for the future but we can also enjoy our downtime.

In living through these challenges with mindfulness we see that we are more than our fears. The negative thoughts that arise at the onset of injury do not need to overcome us. If we can keep things in perspective then this in itself is a source of great pride; not only have we survived an injury but we have improved our resilience and self-confidence for facing future adversity.

What we can learn from dealing with the downtime from running is that there is no solitary area of our lives that offers complete peace, never-ending fitness, health and wellbeing. Running may be something we do that facilitates many aspects of our lives by calming our minds, providing space from daily stress, strengthening our bodies and building physical and mental resilience. Any downtime may reinforce how much we love running and how much we miss it, but if we can manage our recovery mindfully then we may also find that we can live without it – and that can bring its own freedom.

Run
Free

Running is a simple sport; you need nothing more complicated than yourself and a bit of ground to run on. We should feel free to head out of the door at any given moment and just run – on the path, round the park, on or off the trail. But running has become something more; it has taken on an industrial life of its own.

Running is now a challenge set by big events, a financial goal to raise money for charities, a community to be part of; it involves hi-tech watches, shoes and Lycra to adorn ourselves with, and apps to measure our achievements. It is easy to forget how simple it used to be to go out for a run.

There is no doubt that for many runners all of the add-ons provide something – motivation, justification, something to prove that they exist. Capturing a run with technology provides a defence against that cliché of philosophical thought experiments, 'If a tree falls in the forest, and there's nobody around to hear, does it make a sound?' When applied to running, we might ask, 'If I didn't measure it, or time it, does it really count?' For some, this can become an unhealthy obsession; many find it hard to run without a watch or phone to record the event, and some would not even see the point of running without measuring or timing it.

But have we lost something along the way with all these accoutrements? Something that used to be straightforward has become another of life's weights and measures – post-run analysis has become as important as the run itself. Did we hit our targets? Are we improving fast enough? As we run, we are pursued by beeps as we reach mile markers and exceed heart rate limits – it can be hard to run mindfully with all these distractions. And with all the pressure we pile on to reach every target, have we lost sight of the simple pleasure that used to be running?

BACK TO BASICS

Somehow, something that used to be about heading out the door in shorts and a T-shirt has become weighed down by kit and expectation. It is time to consider getting back to basics. Forget about all the technology – set off without a watch or phone, earphone-free, and try to not even have a plan of where you will go.

Think about that for a bit. How does that make you feel about the run? What does your focus become? Without clear goals or measurements the whole focus of the run changes. When you and no one else will know how fast you ran or even how far or for exactly how long, that changes everything. The run becomes about living in the moment, and mindfulness is more easily found; you have nothing to focus on but to engage with your body and your surroundings. You are free to immerse yourself in the meditative art of running.

PURE AND SIMPLE

Sometimes we use our challenges and goals to justify our running, to ourselves and also to others: 'I have to go out for ten miles today or I will never be ready for that half marathon I entered, people have sponsored me, I have to run or I will let them down.' This is a tangible task that we can understand. We are very task-oriented as a species; we rarely prioritize activities that make us feel good.

The importance of our wellbeing is finally being recognized and the power of exercise and mindfulness to maintain it has been identified. You no longer need to justify your running with measurements and beeps. All you need to focus on is your body and the road. The time has come to try running without any of the crutches, to discover what it is to just run. You are free to live in the moment, to enjoy your rhythm and pace, feel your feet on the ground, the air in your lungs and the rhythm of your stride. Engage with your body and your surroundings as you run free.

A Changing
Sense of the World

When we first start running we are not surprised by
the changes that we see in our bodies; a change in
shape is often welcome, not entirely surprising and for
many a key motivation. What is a little less expected
is how running changes our whole interaction with
the world. We see and feel and experience everything
through a new lens and come to know the world in
ways that would have previously been impossible.

When we go running, with a little bit of mindfulness
we awaken all of our senses from our sedentary
hibernation; thinking can be set to one side as we focus

in on seeing, hearing and feeling our way through the world – not just browsing and clicking. Running while fully engaging our senses accentuates the experience.

Our surroundings come alive as we receive the sensory outputs, but the minutiae of the functioning of our environments is largely unavailable to us as humans, with our very basic senses. Watch a dog on a walk and you will be aware that there is a multitude of information to be gleaned with a bit of finer tuning. Nose to the air, ears cocked, they are clearly picking up information that is lost on us. The sounds of bats hunting and even the sap rising though trees in spring have all been captured by the sensitive sound recordings of Chris Watson, a mesmerizing revelation of sound activity in the world as it goes on around us. But fascinating and enlightening as this is, we don't need to have the sensory perception of Superman to be able to experience our world with new clarity.

With sensory awareness, the world we run through is revealed in a new dimension. The landscape is no longer something that we are just passing through and observing; we feel organically part of our world, fully immersed and present. The way that we experience the landscape and our wildlife through our senses can be intense and reminds us that we are actually an integral part of the landscape and how it functions.

CREATING PATHWAYS

As we experience the landscape in this new way we appreciate how we are part of nature but also how we are part of history. As we leave our footprints we are marking our existence on the world; we are marking our point in history. Paths do not make themselves. Our solitary run or the passage of one person in the past has not created the path on which we are running. Footsteps over time, deep into history, have created these paths. We are walking in the footsteps of our ancestors; history precedes every step we take on an established route. Meditate on what draws us to take this path, on what were the motivations of previous

walkers and runners coming this way. Paths are born
of a need – the quickest or easiest route from A to B,
to tend the animals, to trade with others, to carry our
dead. The need for these routes changes our landscape,
scarring the way for future generations. Today's needs
may not be the same, but we follow our senses along
these ways. Reading the natural signposts we become
part of our history, part of the millennia of human
activity that has written these paths for us.

SHARPENING THE SENSES

Unsurprisingly, when we fall in love with running,
we tend to fall in love with the places that we run in.
As we run our heart rate is raised, endorphins course
through our veins, oxygen-rich blood floods our muscles
and brain, we can feel the earth beneath our feet and
the wind in our hair. The world becomes a different
place when you run in it. The relationship we develop
with our surroundings is dynamic – with giving
and taking on both sides. We are physiologically and

psychologically altered by our movement though the world. Our very consciousness is affected by our physical activity.

If we do not mindfully employ the experiences that are filtered through our senses we do ourselves a huge disservice; we cannot experience life to the full in the present moment. When we exercise our bodies they strengthen and develop; we find new capabilities and new limits. The same is true of our senses. As we exercise our senses they too develop, becoming sharper, stronger and more acute. Running changes who you are and how you experience the world in a more profound way than you may ever have thought possible when you first stepped away from the comfort of your home.

Embrace
the Pain

Runners have an unusual relationship with pain. The essence of distance running is that you are pushing yourself to your physical boundary, and that involves encountering pain. As runners, we love and hate that pain. We fear it, but conquering it could be the very reason that we come back time after time. Willingly facing a hard run that we know will be lung rasping, thigh burning and foot-achingly painful gives us the opportunity to feel alive; in our generally seated, air-conditioned lives there is a visceral pleasure in using our bodies in the way that evolution has designed them.

We could take on a sedate run, barely moving our legs and keeping the breathing shallow, but it is rarely enough. Sometimes you head out thinking you'll take it easy but then the rhythm gets going, the metronome begins to move a bit faster and before you know it you are running hard, swinging along, breathing deep in to your core, feeling the ground under your feet and sensing the world around you, fully present in the moment – the very essence of mindfulness.

It seems to be an innate desire we have evolved, the need to push ourselves to test the basic functioning of our bodies. And the inevitable outcome of this is pain, although suffering is avoidable. We cannot escape the pain completely but how we choose to respond to it is down to the individual. If we are frightened of the pain we allow it to have authority and it grows. Alternatively, we can embrace the pain; make friends with it and it becomes less scary.

MIND OVER MATTER

Next time you watch a long race, observe the runners at two points: one just after halfway and the other near the finish. Just after halfway the pain is beginning to kick in; they still have miles to go. The hips sink, the legs are heavy and running form goes out of the window. It is a matter of running survival. Now look again a few miles down the road where the finish line is a tangible reality; those same runners suddenly get a new lease of life. The mental doubts have gone and although the body is still tired there is a new spring in the step and the running form has returned; they are preparing to go swinging happily over the line. So what has changed? The physical condition has not changed – the runners should be more exhausted, no one stopped for a massage and quick lie down – but the whole outlook is different. It's all in the mind.

And that is where mindfulness practice can be so invaluable. You can draw the focus away from the pain and back to the breathing and the cadence, the real essences of running. The pain is not dismissed or ignored but it is reduced to its rightful place. A place of awareness but not power; it is not allowed to get out of control and to overwhelm all other sensations. If we head out knowing that pain is inevitable then we are not taken by surprise, and the pain has less power to overwhelm us. One of the running mantras is to welcome the pain, 'Hello pain, I was expecting you, come run with me'.

LISTEN TO YOUR BODY

Once we can master this approach then our confidence in our ability to embrace the pain of a hard run is immense. Facing the pain is an opportunity to grow – we know it is coming but we don't need to be afraid of it. We can ride those moments of pain without resorting to suffering, and go on to face other challenges that we may have thought impossible. The mental strength achieved in running gives us the self-confidence to face other challenges beyond running; it can help us deal with life.

To push ourselves and endure is a wonderfully life-affirming sign that we are truly human. Employing mindfulness not only enables us to endure more than we probably ever thought was possible, but remaining mindful of ourselves and staying carefully in touch with our bodies as we run also allows us to find that balance between what is possible and what is not. Finding our physical limits is part of the fun; mindlessly running on and on through physical pain is the way to injury, and that is not fun. Retaining a mindful awareness of our bodies and physical sensations keeps us in touch with minor niggles and identifies when they became causes for concern. Sometimes the sensible option is to stop.

The Running
Community

Running can be the ultimate in solitary activities, the cliché of the loneliness of the long-distance runner. Battling inner demons, the elements and the world in general reflects many people's running experience. There is great freedom and flexibility in running alone, and achieving a mindful focus may feel easiest on solo runs, but there is also huge merit in the camaraderie of the running community.

BREAKING DOWN SOCIAL BARRIERS

Running communities come in all shapes and sizes –
it may be just a single running buddy in your lunch
hour, a small group getting together for training runs
or a whole running club with organized events, or it
may be the virtual community formed by social network
apps connecting millions of runners online who map,
measure and share their running experiences.

Whatever the running community, there are certain
universal features that I love. Running can be one of
the best social levellers I know, which is just as good
for the soul as it is for the society. Anxiety and an array
of other mental and physical ailments have been linked
to social inequality. Once we start to run, however,
the usual social stratification is suspended. A different
hierarchy may exist based on our running capabilities,
but running provides the opportunity to transcend the
usual social boundaries and develop close relationships
between different educational backgrounds, nationalities,
religions and income groups.

FORGING FRIENDSHIPS

The potential for developing cohesion and building communities through running has been recognized and explored in many parts of the world to help integrate disparate groups. It can draw refugees and displaced individuals into their new lives and create community cohesion in a socially egalitarian setting.

Once we leave our daily lives behind and start to think about running, we anticipate the joy of the physical activity. Our focus is removed from our usual friendships and interactions, and we move beyond the barriers that we put up in our everyday life. It seems that when we run and exist in the moment we are able to leave our social hang-ups and emotional baggage behind. Unlikely friendships can be forged and meaningless barriers broken down. Many running communities rapidly extend beyond the weekly run; social events, organized races, training challenges, holidays and other opportunities for greater involvement in the running world can be pursued.

GAINING PERSPECTIVE

By employing our mindfulness practices as we run, we come to know ourselves really well; this self-awareness leads to an unconditional acceptance of ourselves just as we are. Running and communicating mindfully with others can open our eyes to new ways of thinking, and we can grow our experiences faster and more widely when we add them to those of others, amplifying the mindful experience. Through the combined experiences of a group of runners we can develop our individual concept of self-awareness and learn to be more aware and unconditionally accepting of others as well. Learning to accept people just as they are develops a greater tolerance to others, leading to less social stress and anxiety.

As we run mindfully we can also come face-to-face with ourselves in quite an exposing way. Difficult emotions may arise which can threaten to overwhelm us. Within a running community, we are surrounded by others facing the same emotions. The normalization of the experience and the empathy of a fellow runner leads to understanding and support. Accepting and even laughing at our defeats allows us to put them in perspective and move past them more readily.

When you share your run with others, you will find that you are not alone. Everyone goes through the same physical and emotional cycles, experiencing moments of pleasure and pain, elation and dejection, motivation and antipathy. Being with others who are facing the same challenges and finding themselves in the same position is reaffirming; it reinforces your own experiences and reassures you that they are quite normal.

The Ageing Runner

Our bodies are clocks marking the passage of time, slowly but surely, and the inevitability of our physical decline can sometimes be hard to accept.

EMBRACING CHANGE

Controlling time is not an option. We may not be happy about it but it is beyond our control; like the weather, railing against it gets us nowhere. It is life and if we fail to reach some acceptance then we risk an emotional decline into regret and loss. But all is not lost. The first signs of physical niggles and slipping times do not need to signal the beginning of the end of our running. The oldest big-city marathon runners are often in their eighties and nineties – there's a good chance that we can keep running until we drop.

Approaching our running mindfully equips us to deal better with the changes inherent in the ageing runner. There are many positives to be gained from these changes that may initially seem disconcerting. Over the years of maintaining a mindful awareness of our bodies we will have accumulated a deep understanding of our responses to external stimuli – how we cope with the ups and downs of the route, a variety of weathers, mixed terrain and the inevitable mental and physical toll all this takes. We will be aware of how our bodies respond to these conditions and will be able to adapt our recovery and training to minimize the negative impact on our bodies. As we get older we learn how to train smarter, not harder, to maintain our levels of performance.

FINDING A NEW FOCUS

Times provide the impetus for many runners. The inevitability of the passage of time is matched by the inevitability of declining running times. As hard as you fight it, when you reach a certain point it is most unlikely you will ever run the way you used to and achieve the times that you reached as a younger runner. On the face of it, it may not be one of our happier realities, but remember those wise words of William Bruce Cameron, 'not everything that counts can be counted'. Times are not everything.

Once we accept that times are not the be all and end all of running then we release ourselves into a whole world of running opportunities. Although our initial response to slowing down may be dissatisfaction, on further reflection we may realize there are positives in the change of focus. One of the joys of the ageing runner is releasing some of the pressure to perform; it makes sense to change the focus and find new goals in our running lives. There are many immeasurable pleasures and benefits of running that are frequently overlooked. For example, we can still maintain an involvement in races and regular training but now the focus may be on the physical sensation of the run, the setting, the atmosphere of a challenge shared and the spectacle of an event – it actually becomes more meaningful when you can enjoy yourself and find a feeling of pride in your performance that comes from a more intangible goal.

There may come a time that we can no longer run at all. If we do not run mindfully now then we are cheating ourselves of the ability to enjoy our running into our dotage. If, however, we have spent our running lives well, savouring the moments rather than frittering them away, we will have stored up memories for the future. Moments lived mindfully live on forever, written into our memories, available to be read and reread.

The physical and mental benefits of running are too great to throw away with a drop in times and aching limbs; the connectivity with our bodies and the wider world provides benefits in increased mobility, freedom, camaraderie and a positive outlook on life that can provide a route to happy ageing.

The benefits of mindful running throughout our lives are great but perhaps the time to really reap the rewards will come in our older age. Be kind to your future self and focus on your mindful running now – you will thank yourself for it. The longevity of the mindful runner is such that you should be able to keep running into old age with as much fulfilment and enjoyment as your younger running self. There is no need to let go of our abilities and our vitality just because we are not the runners we used to be. We can still be runners and we can still enjoy our moments on the road – possibly even more than we used to.

Change
Your Mind

As runners, we all recognize the general feeling of wellbeing that pervades after a good run. Mindful running can cultivate feelings of peace, contentment and gratitude, which can do wonders for elevating our mood and building our self-confidence.

CLINGING TO NEGATIVITY

However, sometimes our subconscious still conspires to undermine these positive emotions. We are creatures of habit and one particularly human trait is to dwell on the negative. Following well-worn patterns of thought, we create self-fulfilling prophecies with the automatic or unconscious thoughts that dominate our minds, just below our level of awareness. These unconscious thoughts become the stories we tell ourselves over and over until they become so ingrained that they feel as if they are part of our identity. Without even being aware of it, we limit ourselves with such unconscious thoughts as, 'I'm not good enough to do that race', or 'I would be a real runner if only I had more time for it'.

These same patterns of thought tend to pervade throughout our lives and can be detrimental to our progress. As much as we don't like it, it is easier to cling to negativity than to really believe we can do something – but it is necessary for us to believe to be able to achieve. It is one of life's conundrums.

REWRITE THE SCRIPT

The wonderful opportunity that mindfulness brings is that it allows us to notice these negative thoughts and replace them with a more positive, deep-seated state of mind. As we run mindfully we develop an awareness of our thoughts. We develop the ability to identify that thoughts are just that – thoughts. We appreciate that they do not need to define us; they come and go and we can therefore reduce the power that they exert over us and the reliance that we develop on them. This way, we can rewrite our story, building a belief in ourselves and supporting a narrative in which we have the capacity to be a capable, confident and strong runner. This creates possibilities to extend ourselves and opens up doors for new adventures and experiences that had previously been closed to us.

But running does not only allow us to rewrite a more positive approach to life, it also allows us to unravel all kinds of mental tangles and to be more receptive to new ideas. We can use running as a tool to right the mental wrongs that develop in everyday life; running gives us a chance to reset our day.

WELCOMING CHANGE

Our natural habit-forming tendencies and the need to simplify our complex lives means that we are not overly receptive to suggestions that require change. Through our need to simplify we follow the same patterns of behaviour and thoughts every day. To a given set of questions, we will usually have set responses. When we are challenged to rethink our approach we don't like it. By continually repeating our well-worn patterns of thought and behaviour we have put up mental barriers to new ideas. A new approach is usually instantly dismissed and rejected – backed up by our history of set thought patterns. This approach to life is actually a survival instinct but sometimes we need to consider new ideas and take on board change.

Our minds have to be loose and relaxed to allow new thoughts and approaches in. Running provides some mental space, allowing our minds to enter a place where thoughts are free-flowing, unstructured and unfocused. As we run along, striding though the world, the breeze on our skin, we release ourselves from our usual constraints and the mind flies with the body. As we loosen our hold on our mind we begin to free-associate.

Without censorship we allow thoughts to come and go, often unrelated or seemingly irrelevant and random. There is a great opportunity to reset our minds to create new pathways and break down those well-worn patterns of thought. A new mindset and key insights can arrive when we allow our minds some space and flexibility to work.

New concepts that we rush to reject and intractable problems that arise can usually be accommodated and unsnarled by a run. You can use this for yourself, but it also holds true for others. If you want to suggest a change to a boss or loved one, the best time to put forward a new idea is just before they go for a run – but don't ask for the answer until they come back!

The Charitable Runner

So you've decided to challenge yourself and you've entered a big race. You've been putting in the miles, following a training schedule that you've approached mindfully, stretching and resting as much as running. The big day is getting ever nearer and you are excited and nervous in equal measure. Then people start to ask why you have chosen to do it.

Training for a big run takes a lot of time and commitment. It impinges on our everyday life and therefore on our families and friends; many hours are spent pounding along the footpaths and trails in pursuit of the fitness required to complete a major run. We know the benefits of running for our wellbeing, and the desire to challenge ourselves for that big run is an inevitable progression of the running bug. To discover within ourselves the mental and physical strength to complete a major distance is life-changing. But there's more to it: the 'big race' can open up even more opportunities than overcoming the physical and mental challenge it presents.

MAKING A CONNECTION

While mindfulness starts with our personal state of mind, practitioners of mindfulness soon discover that alongside the development of our personal awareness also comes an awareness of others. With awareness comes the desire for connection. As you run with this consciousness, picture yourself on your big day. Shoulder to shoulder you take on the challenge; falling into step with your fellow runners you find that you develop a mindful recognition of your time on earth together, a greater perception of the connection we all share, that together we are all souls sharing the same space on earth. The ability to choose a charitable cause to run for enables us to express the connectivity with the wider world that we feel.

TAKING A POSITIVE STEP

Your choice of charity can be used as an opportunity to express yourself. Maybe through your own personal interests or connections you can choose a charity that is of particular personal significance; you may even declare your support for a particular charity as part of a healing process. Personal tragedies and challenges from mental health, illness, injury and bereavement are inevitable at some point in most of our lives. Choosing a charity can be a way of thanking and funding those organizations which provide support, research or treatment for your particular challenge. Raising money in relation to a negative experience in your life can also feel like a positive step in your own healing. Doing something to fight back and not letting life get you down can be an amazingly positive experience.

Whichever good cause you support, it is a great way to make a connection with people that you have never even met. When you choose to run for others you find that you step into their shoes, and as you run with them you become mindful of their challenges, you feel a greater connection to others and through your running you bond to the wider world.

On a personal, practical note, raising money to help others can provide useful additional motivation. Every step you take is working towards a better future for someone else – during those moments when your resilience is stretched to the extreme, these thoughts drive you on. When you start fundraising you become part of another community; wearing their T-shirt brings more encouragement from their supporters and can help carry you along with a wave of positivity. Since running can isolate you for hours from family and friends, involving them in the event through donations can help to bring them along on the run with you. They may have a particular bond with the charity you have chosen and it provides another avenue for them to appreciate the effort you are putting into this big event.

So, picture yourself on your big run: breath in, breath out, footstep after footstep, arm-swing after arm-swing, fully in the moment, the roar of the crowds carrying you along, everyone involved in their own little sphere of personal challenge but at the same time a challenge shared. You feel a sense of pride and quiet happiness at what you are achieving. The shared empathy that comes from being part of a greater body of action enables you to connect in action and work for humanity.

Running
Rituals

As humans we are creatures of habit; we cope best when we work with the cycles of our existence. To manage the uncertainty in our lives we create patterns and rhythms, adopting comforting and helpful rituals along the way. Historically, rituals have formed the basis of our cultural and religious practices, marking the passage of time and life's milestones – ceremonies of life, death and marriage. Without thought we all move and work to our annual rhythms, superimposed with seasonal rituals and overlain by our cultural and spiritual interpretation. This collective understanding brings communities together and provides the structure which we all understand and binds us together.

On a shorter timescale, we recreate these same patterns and rhythms in our lives to help us to manage our daily cycles. The daily rituals we perform are important to our health and happiness. These may be habits that we have subconsciously fallen into or that we have learned and adopted mindfully. Over time they become a part of our lives, a part of ourselves, an affirming part of our identity and individuality.

Runners can be quite quirky in their rituals. Most runners are susceptible to the idea of certain warm-up routines and motivational music, wearing lucky socks, consuming certain pre-run drinks and snacks – however large or small, practical or crazy, every runner has their own unbreakable and carefully devised rituals.

MENTAL PREPARATION

Running can be a challenge; it happens in the mind as much as in the body. How we prepare mentally is as important as how we prepare physically, and while most runners tend to focus on their form, pace and distance, the mental strength that feeling prepared gives us is almost as important as actually being physically ready for the run. While these habits may have come from a place of mindful awareness and consideration, over time they can become degraded and often take on the mantle of mindless routine and even superstition. They can still be important in this form, providing a rhythm and focus to our preparations that keeps us calm and on track. The danger with routines carried out mindlessly, however, is that their presence becomes more important than what they provide us with. We can become overly dependent on the need to complete an aspect of our routine, and if for some reason we can't, this becomes detrimental to our mental preparation.

By retaining a mindful focus in our rituals, we can keep them as a positive element in our running preparation. In moments of uncertainty and stress, they can bring familiarity and a sense of purpose which helps us to stay grounded, providing a reassuring rhythm to an unsettling day.

A mindful awareness can start before we even lace up our shoes. We all know that running can be hard. If we are not mentally primed, the pain can take us by surprise and can be hard to endure. Making part of our pre-run routine a conscious exercise in mindfulness can provide tangible benefits. Breathing exercises and body scans can help to ground us in our bodies and bring us fully into the present. Being aware of our physical and mental state primes us for the challenge ahead. The effect can be calming, particularly on race days when anxiety threatens to override our groundwork.

BUILDING CONFIDENCE

With mindful routines, we can feel confident that everything is in place for our best efforts. To perform our best we need to find a balance between being complacent and succumbing to the anxiety that threatens to engulf us. Our rituals can help to ensure that we are excited and in the zone, but relaxed – the perfect state for optimum performance.

Often, the build-up to a long training run requires a similar preparation to a long race. We learn what we like and what works for us. We feel confident that we are in the best state to take on the challenge. When things start to get tough, the fact that we know we are wearing our comfortable socks and we have eaten oatmeal two hours beforehand helps us to know that we are in the best place mentally and physically and that we have within us what it takes to achieve our goal.

As you prepare for your next run, approach your rituals in a mindful way; be aware of how you are grounding yourself and building your physical and mental preparedness for the challenge ahead. Notice as you enter into a state of excited relaxation, ready to get in the zone. By practising mindfulness before you run, you can improve your performance – so carry out your rituals mindfully and reassure yourself that you are in the best place to succeed.

Short
&
Sweet

It is widely observed that the current approach to life is one where we always want more and faster, and when it comes to running this is no different.

Shireen Bailey, a British Olympic 800 m and 1500 m runner in the 1980s, is still frequently asked what the furthest distance is that she has run. No matter that Shireen ran incredibly fast or that almost forty years on from her championship days she is still enjoying her running and passing that love on to other runners, she always encounters disappointment when people hear that she rarely hits double figures.

But more is not always better. We do not need to get caught up in a distance-running arms-race where 10 km trumps 5 km, marathon trumps half-marathon and ultra-marathons trump them all.

SEIZE THE MOMENT

Some days there simply is not enough time to go out for hours on end; we may only have time for a short twenty-minute loop and this is no less valid than a much longer run. Mindfulness is about accepting what we have in our present moment as being enough. This means we accept the compromises and limitations of ourselves and our situations and we make the best of what is on offer. Some people cannot get enough time for even a short run during their busy working week; some people live in areas with such bad air pollution that they would not even risk running outside for twenty minutes. Some days you just have to take what is on offer. There are many times that a short run has revealed unexpected joys and moments of clarity and interest in my life. So take those precious twenty minutes of free time, grab the opportunity with both hands and get out there.

Anything is better than nothing when it comes to time out on a run, and when approached mindfully, going for a quick run can be as rewarding as a two-hour long-distance epic. Many mindfulness exercises start with just a ten-minute session; there is no set amount of time required for a stress-busting, mind-calming, bliss-finding mobile meditation. There is no need to run for hours to clear your mind, still your anxieties and enjoy a bit of freedom.

A VITAL PART OF TRAINING

Another advantage of the short run is that it is easier to be motivated to fit one into your schedule and more realistic than trying to squeeze in an hour. Long runs can be overwhelming; some days it's hard to get out of the door, even when you know you will feel better if you do. A short, bite-sized run just seems more manageable and is a good place to start. Some days, your plan may spontaneously change and a short run may develop into a much longer outing.

One of the common hazards faced by runners is that, intent on making improvements, they will over-train. A short run brings physical and mental benefits as well as being easier to fit into our busy lives. Understanding these benefits can not only help the mindful runner accept them into their routine but positively appreciate the value they can bring. Long runs every day risk overuse injuries. It is important to mix up our training to include some days of shorter runs as well as some rest days. If you don't have time for a long run make a positive of it, ease off or even take it as a rest day.

To improve our speed we need to mix in some interval sessions. A variety of run lengths is actually recommended to optimize our training. While a long distance may be the ultimate goal it's important to mix in some short, fast runs, some hill work and some interval training. These are the runs that will make you faster and enable you to pick up the pace on the long ones. Take a short-run day and mix it up. Meet up with friends and do some intervals, work hard, and even though you won't be able to stay out for too long, there's no quicker way to get fit.

If it looks like being a short-run day, don't get upset about it; take a moment of mindfulness and reassess the situation. Take it in your stride, thank your lucky stars for whatever you can do and make the most of it.

Making
Good Choices

Life is like the best kind of running: the route
is not straight and predetermined, every step of
the way we meet twists and turns, and there are
decisions to be made. Some are large and some
small – do we step on the stone or the mud,
or even in the middle of the puddle? Do we
cross the road here or further on? Do we go
up the hill or along the stream?

WHICH PATH DO WE CHOOSE?

We make many decisions without much conscious
thought. Orange juice or apple juice? Walk, cycle or
drive? Some decisions are made based on the way

we are feeling that day, a follow-your-heart intuitive reaction. Other decisions involve a less emotional, more reasoned response based on the available data and a logical thought process. Many decisions employ a mixture of the two.

Sometimes we can get stuck. We just can't seem to make a decision. We go round and round in circles, never reaching an answer. This may be because the decision to be made has life-changing implications, but sometimes we just find ourselves stymied because we have too many options, and even the smallest decision becomes a problem. As we go round and round, our head gets in a spin and we soon become overwhelmed.

The freedom of personal choice is perhaps the most fundamental of human rights. To make good choices for ourselves in life we need to understand what kind of person we are, what kind of person we want to be and how we want to be seen by others. We need to know ourselves. If we do not know ourselves well, then decision-making becomes a very tricky task. We are constantly redefining ourselves, which takes huge amounts of energy and can be an emotional process. The responsibility of making a decision can seem on one hand empowering but on the other hand terrifying.

CREATING CLARITY

Mindful running can help with making decisions because when we run mindfully, we learn a lot about ourselves. You may think that you know yourself well already but every day we are bombarded with a vast amount of information from the media and the people we talk to; we are exposed to many other people's values and messages. Whether it is specifically targeted to influence us or not (and much of it is), it all has an impact on the decisions that we make in everyday life. It can add to our confusion when conflicting external values trip up our internal priorities.

Going off for a run removes us from most of the external influences that threaten to divert us from our true path. Running creates a certain measure of calm, which gives us some space and time. As we run, we observe and acknowledge thoughts as they come and go; we become familiar with our thought processes. We also notice our feelings. Identifying and acknowledging the difference between thinking and feeling allows us to understand what is fundamental to us and what is just a passing thought. We learn much about our own values and priorities, and we open ourselves up to our own truths, making it easier to see what is really important to us, what our real objectives are. This means that when decisions need to be made, we have that framework and understanding of who we are, and it is easier to reach the right decision for ourselves.

This may work for many decisions but sometimes the decision is just too great; it is a messy, sticky mass of uncertainty and turmoil. By bringing you closer to yourself with compassion, mindful running can help you to tolerate and be kind to the uncertainty within you. Often there are no right or wrong answers, and even if there are, everyone gets it wrong sometimes. By recognizing the imperfections within yourself and the impossibility of an error-free life, you can achieve a sense of self-acceptance.

The whole process of decision-making can be considerably less traumatic when we approach it with mindfulness. We become more tolerant of uncertainty and are happier to make decisions even in the face of a number of unknowns. When you are happy with the decision-making process you are also more likely to follow through and act on the decisions you have made – this positive affirmation reinforces the process and makes it easier next time.

Switch Off
& Recharge

It has been estimated that we consume about three times the amount of information that we did in the 1960s. Our world today is 'always on'. With the World Wide Web at our fingertips there is never any need to be without that moment-by-moment input of knowledge.

The benefits of this connectivity may be great but there are downsides too. There are many studies and much anecdotal evidence that supports our personal intuition and tells us that too much time spent with technological devices takes its toll. Even tech giants such as Google, Apple and Yahoo have recognized the downsides of constantly being 'on' and are taking steps to help their employees by providing onsite meditation classes to encourage downtime, even as they perpetuate the 'always on' experience.

But why is being 'always on' such a problem? Surveys have shown that we find it hard to ignore that beep that announces something landing on our phones; even when we are involved in other fun activities, we will become distracted and feel the need to check. Strangely, we are not rewarded with a good feeling when we do respond. In a survey by meQuilibrium, over sixty per cent of respondents said they feel jealous, depressed or sad after checking updates on social media, and seventy percent of people recognized that their devices contribute to stress in their lives.

THREE TYPES OF ATTENTION

The kind of brain activity we use when we engage in screen time is one of a range of different types of attention that we have.

The first, most basic, type is involuntary attention, which is when our brain responds to an outside stimulus without the need for conscious thought. For example, dropping our phone results in an involuntary response – putting out our hands to try to catch it.

A second type of attention is directed attention. This is when our brain is engaged and directed towards a certain stimulus that is holding our attention. Studying, reading, watching TV, even flicking through social media – all employ directed attention and require concentration. Our concentration takes energy and is therefore a finite resource; if it is not replenished it results in mental fatigue. Like our phone batteries, it wears out and needs recharging.

The third type of attention is soft fascination. Soft fascination is typified by an effortless, meandering free-form of thought often mediated by the natural environment and maximized by mindfulness. Our brains are observing what is going on around us, thoughts come and go, and while we are observing our surroundings with a relaxed and soft focus, our mental batteries are being recharged.

SWITCHING OFF

When we switch off our electronic devices and run mindfully (particularly in natural environments) then we accelerate our minds into soft fascination; by providing some space from directed attention, we are helping our minds to switch off, too. Spending time in this soft fascination is important for healthy mental functioning and is being increasingly squeezed out by the widely accessible connectivity and ubiquitous nature of our devices.

One of the reasons that mindfulness is so successful in calming and relaxing us is that our brains are actually incapable of focusing on two things at once. This is why research shows us again and again that multi-tasking is not as efficient as focusing on one task at a time, no matter what we may think. As we run mindfully, we practise focusing on the present – we stay in the moment and as we do this we inhibit our mind from thinking about all those other stimulants and anxiety-inducing elements of our lives.

We are so conditioned to being constantly stimulated in life that some runners find they get bored, or expect to get bored, and they choose to listen to music or podcasts as they run. Runners who switch off for a while learn to focus their attention mindfully on their senses and begin to pick up the more subtle sights and sounds and sensations of the real world – like food without flavourings, the subtleties of the natural flavours reveal themselves. If we stay connected to our devices as we run, we are depriving ourselves of the opportunity to connect to ourselves and our surroundings, but we are also depriving ourselves of some important recharging time. So give it a go; give yourself a break, switch off and recharge.

ACKNOWLEDGEMENTS

Thank you to Monica, Tom, Elizabeth and all at Leaping
Hare for their hard work in the production of this book.
For their unfailing enthusiasm and mutual encouragement,
I would like to thank my fellow runners at the Fit Hub and
Hawthorn's, and particularly our coach, Shireen, for her clear
enjoyment in our heavy breathing and pain. I would also
like to thank Caroline, Vanessa and Dunc for their company
and fun; Anousha, Poppy, Thea and Lottie, who either left me
behind long ago or threaten to do so soon; and of course,
Alfie and Fifa for their copious black hair and mud.

Running clubs sustain running communities the world over,
so a big shout out to everyone at my local club,
Reigate Priory, and to all running clubs. Without the
dedication of the coaches, parents and enthusiasts who
support, motivate and enrich the global running community
the running world would be so much poorer.